EASY GUITAR
WITH NOTES & TAB

Best Children's

T0055772

ISBN 978-1-4803-4516-4

HAL•LEONARD® CORPORATION

7777 W. BLUEMOUND RD. P.O. BOX 13819 MILWAUKEE, WI 53213

Visit Hal Leonard Online at
www.halleonard.com

Contents

STRUM AND PICK PATTERNS

This chart contains the suggested strum and pick patterns that are referred to by number at the beginning
of each song in this book. The symbols ⊓ and ∨ in the strum patterns refer to down and up strokes, respectively.
The letters in the pick patterns indicate which right-hand fingers play which strings.

p = thumb
i = index finger
m = middle finger
a = ring finger

For example; Pick Pattern 2
is played: thumb - index - middle - ring

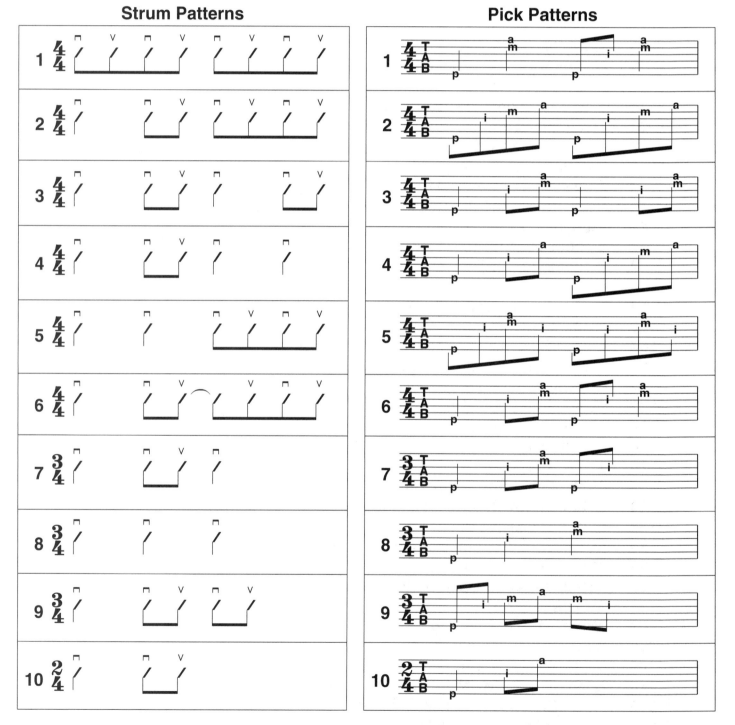

Strum Patterns

Pick Patterns

You can use the 3/4 Strum and Pick Patterns in songs written in compound meter (6/8, 9/8, 12/8, etc.).
For example, you can accompany a song in 6/8 by playing the 3/4 pattern twice in each measure.
The 4/4 Strum and Pick Patterns can be used for songs written in cut time (¢) by doubling the note
time values in the patterns. Each pattern would therefore last two measures in cut time.

Addams Family Theme

Theme from the TV Show and Movie

Music and Lyrics by Vic Mizzy

Additional Lyrics

2. Their house is a museum,
   Where people come to see 'um.
   They're really are a screeum,
   The Addams Family.

3. So get a witches shawl on,
   A broom stick you can crawl on.
   We're gonna pay a call on,
   The Addams Family.

Alley Cat Song

Words by Jack Harlen
Music by Frank Bjorn

*Lyrics in italics are spoken throughout.

leaves 'em. (mee - ow.) That's what Cat - sa - no - va does.

Verse

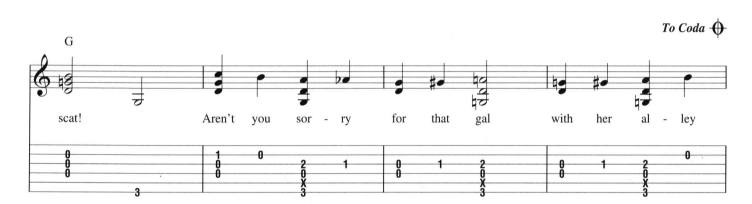

3., 6. It's no way to treat a pal, she should tell him,

To Coda ⊕

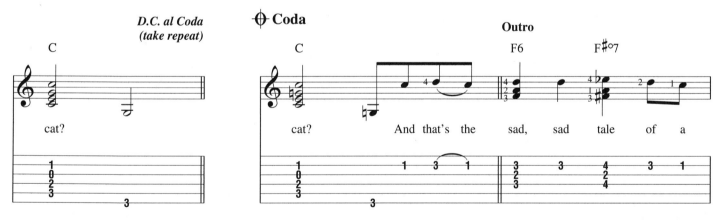

scat! Aren't you sor - ry for that gal with her al - ley

D.C. al Coda (take repeat)   ⊕ **Coda**   **Outro**

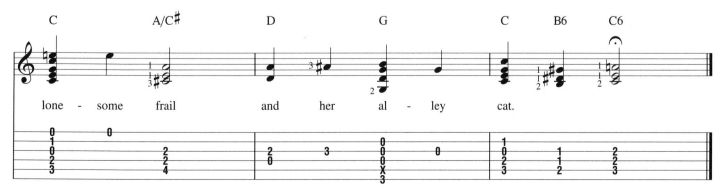

cat?   cat? And that's the sad, sad tale of a

lone - some frail and her al - ley cat.

Any Dream Will Do

from JOSEPH AND THE AMAZING TECHNICOLOR® DREAMCOAT

Music by Andrew Lloyd Webber
Lyrics by Tim Rice

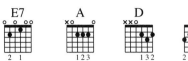

Strum Pattern: 3, 4
Pick Pattern: 3, 4

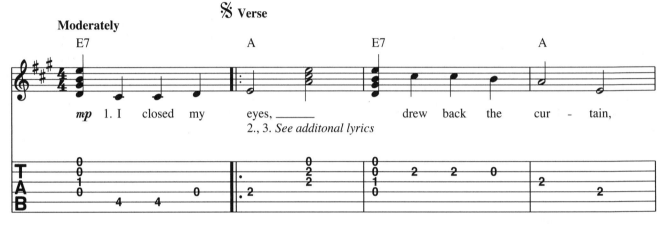

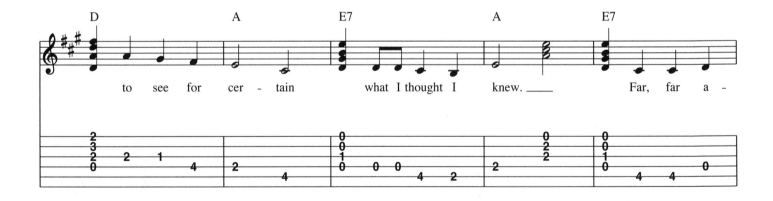

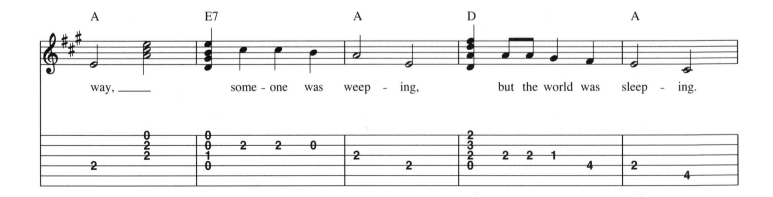

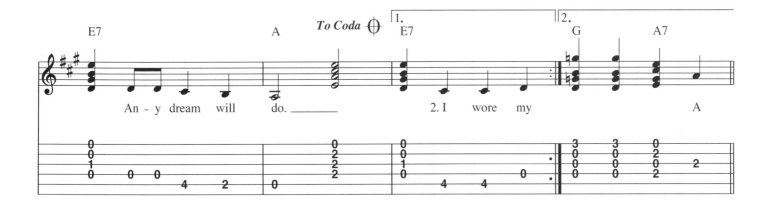

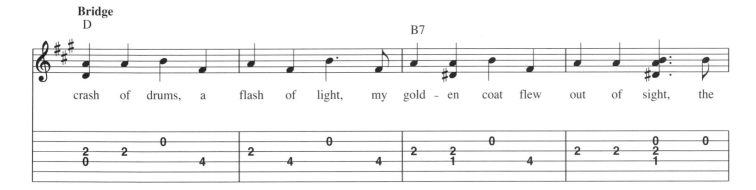

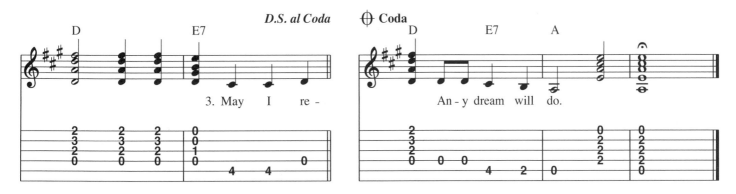

Additional Lyrics

2. I wore my coat with golden lining,
   Bright colours shining, wonderful and new.
   And in the East the dawn was breaking,
   The world was waking, any dream will do.

3. May I return to the beginning,
   The light is dimming and the dream is too.
   The world and I we are still waiting,
   Still hesitating, any dream will do.

Baby Mine

Words by Ned Washington
Music by Frank Churchill

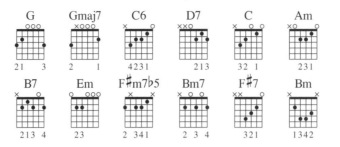

Strum Pattern: 3
Pick Pattern: 3

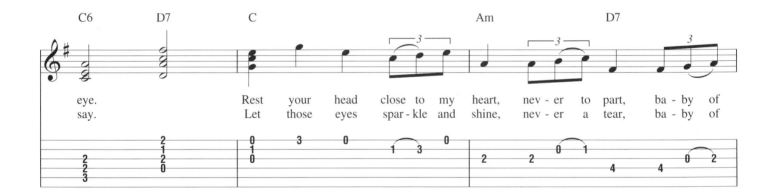

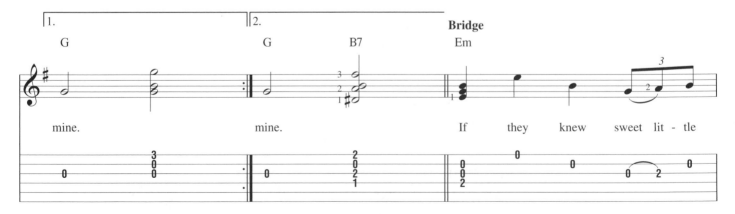

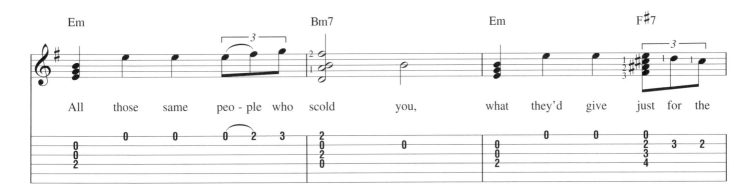

Verse

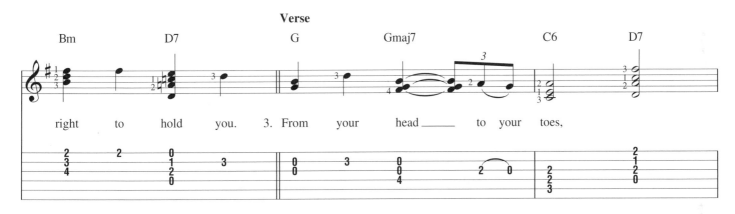

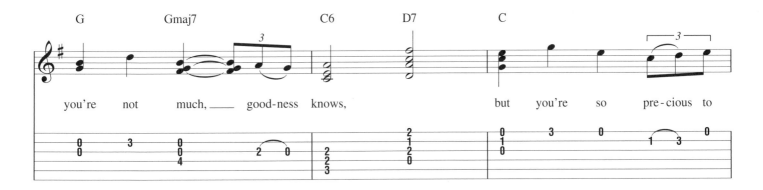

Bein' Green

Words and Music by Joe Raposo

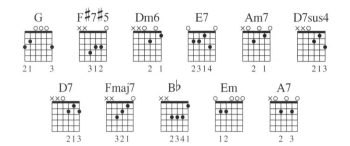

Strum Pattern: 5
Pick Pattern: 5

Verse
Moderately slow

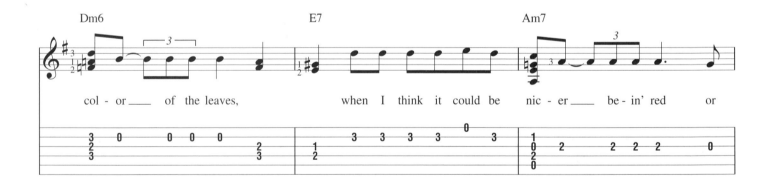

1. It's not that eas - y ___ be - in' green, hav - ing to spend each day the

col - or ___ of the leaves, when I think it could be nic - er ___ be - in' red or

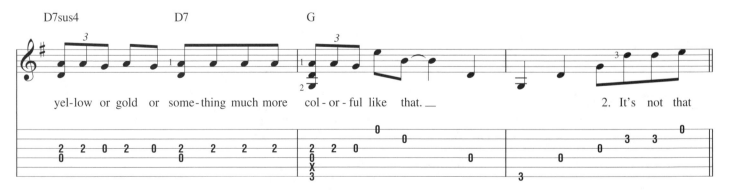

yel - low or gold or some - thing much more col - or - ful like that. ___ 2. It's not that

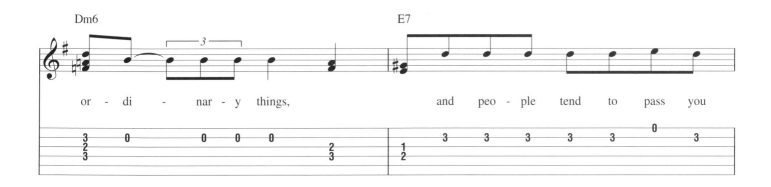

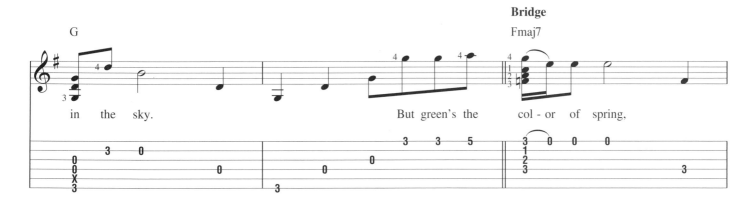

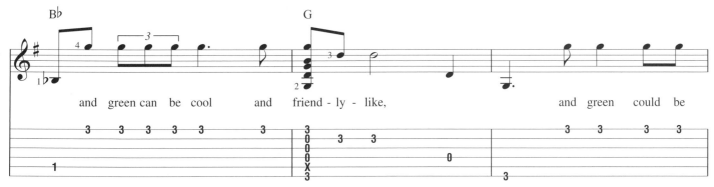

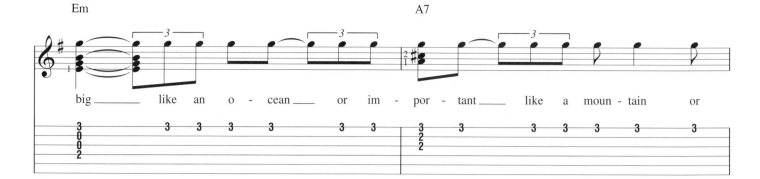

big___ like an o - cean___ or im - por - tant___ like a moun - tain or

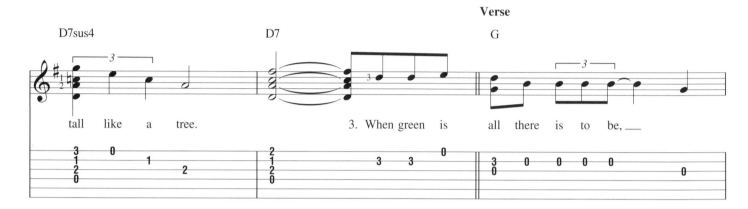

tall like a tree.   3. When green is   all there is to be, ___

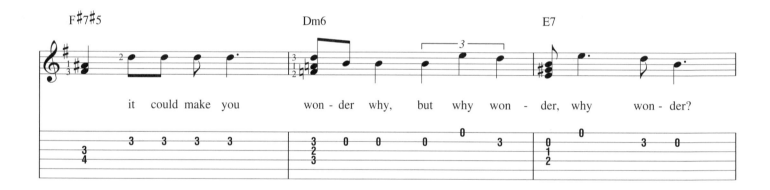

it could make you   won - der why,   but why won - der, why   won - der?

I'm green,   and it - 'll do fine,   and it's beau - ti - ful,

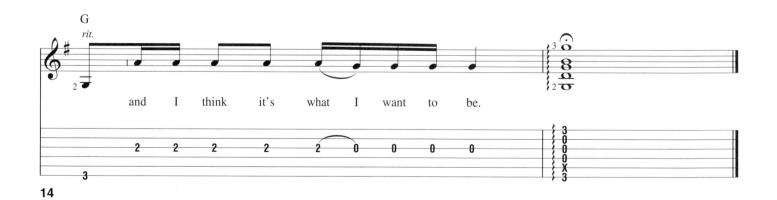

and I think it's   what I want to be.

Can You Feel the Love Tonight

from Walt Disney Pictures' THE LION KING

Music by Elton John
Lyrics by Tim Rice

*Tune down 1 step:
(low to high) D-G-C-F-A-D

Strum Pattern: 4
Pick Pattern: 4

*Optional: To match recording, tune down 1 step.

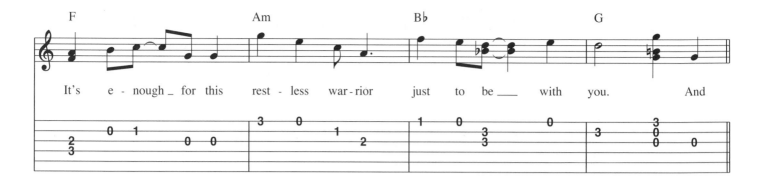

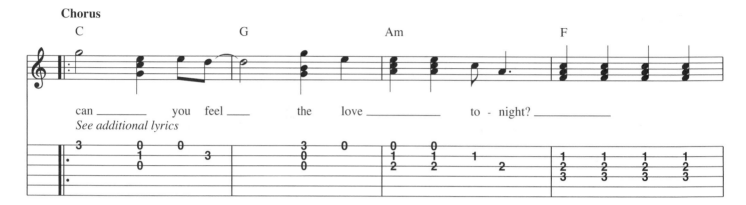

Chorus

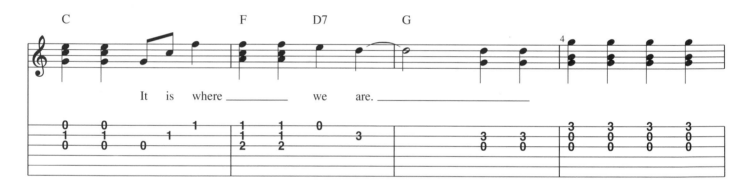

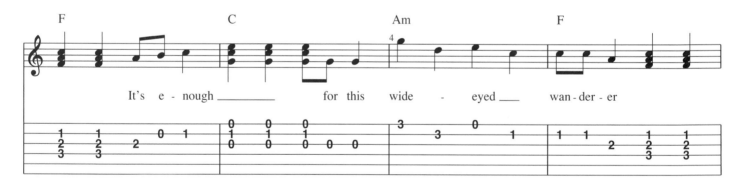

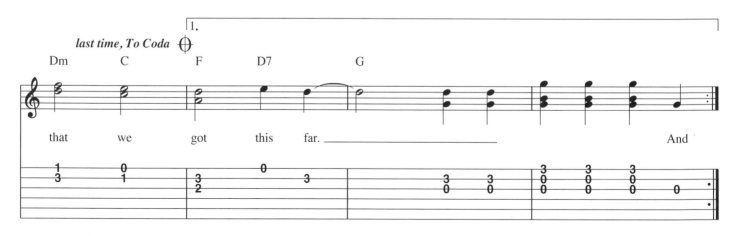

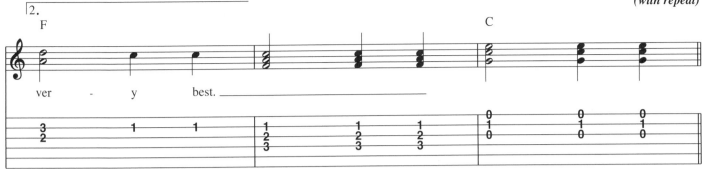

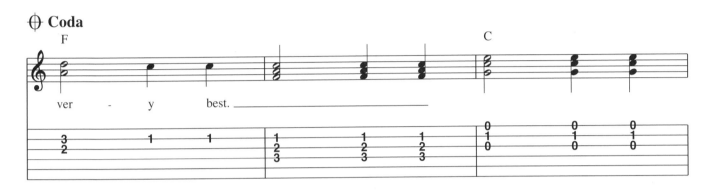

Additional Lyrics

2. There's a time for ev'ryone,
If they only learn
That the twisting kaleidoscope
Moves us all in turn.
There's a rhyme and reason
To the wild outdoors
When the heart of this star-crossed voyager
Beats in time with yours.

Chorus And can you feel the love tonight,
How it's laid to rest?
It's enough to make kings and vagabonds
Believe the very best.

Bob the Builder
"Intro Theme Song"

Words and Music by Paul Joyce

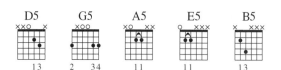

Strum Pattern: 3
Pick Pattern: 3

Chorus
Moderately fast

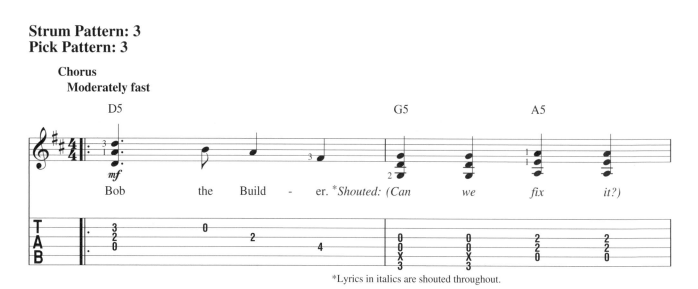

*Lyrics in italics are shouted throughout.

Verse

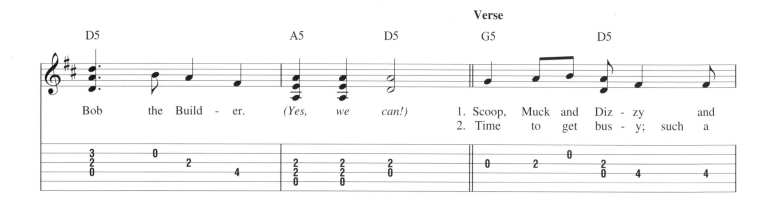

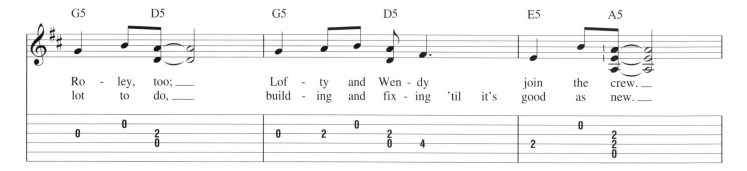

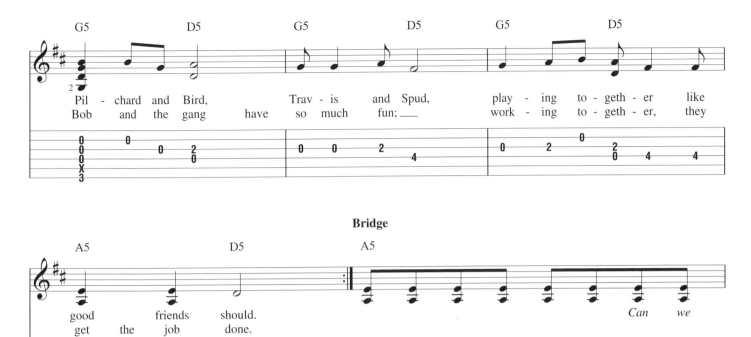

Pil - chard and Bird, Trav - is and Spud, play - ing to - geth - er like
Bob and the gang have so much fun; ___ work - ing to - geth - er, like they

Bridge

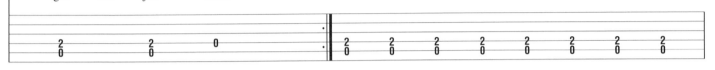

good friends should. Can we
get the job done.

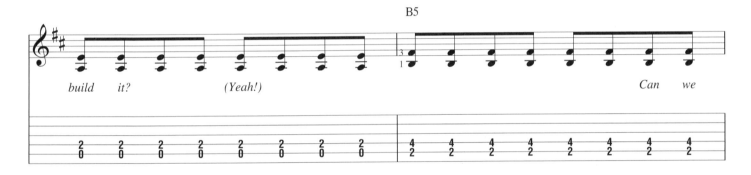

build it? (Yeah!) Can we

Outro-Chorus

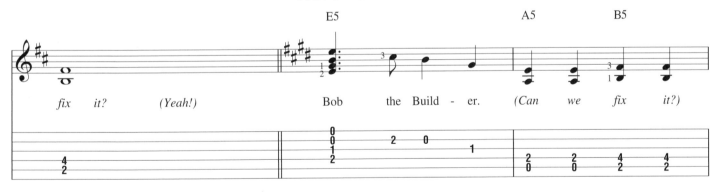

fix it? (Yeah!) Bob the Build - er. (Can we fix it?)

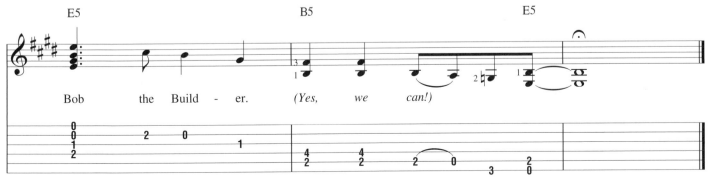

Bob the Build - er. (Yes, we can!)

"C" Is for Cookie

Words and Music by Joe Raposo

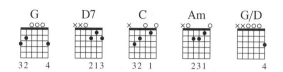

Strum Pattern: 4
Pick Pattern: 1

Intro
Moderately

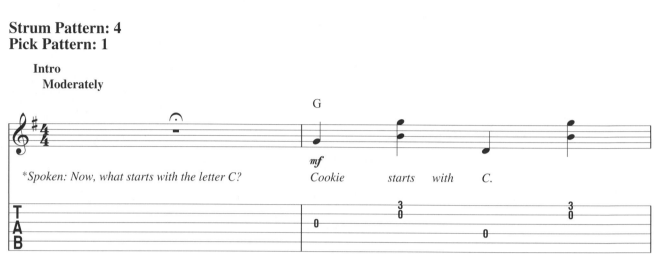

Spoken: Now, what starts with the letter C? Cookie starts with C.

*Lyrics in italics are spoken throughout.

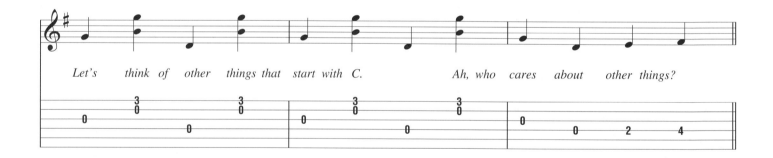

Let's think of other things that start with C. Ah, who cares about other things?

Verse

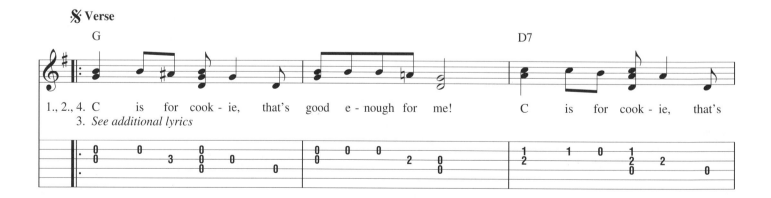

1., 2., 4. C is for cook-ie, that's good e-nough for me! C is for cook-ie, that's
3. *See additional lyrics*

good e-nough for me! C is for cook-ie, that's good e-nough for me! Oh,

4th time, To Coda ⊕ | 1.

D.S. al Coda
(take repeat)

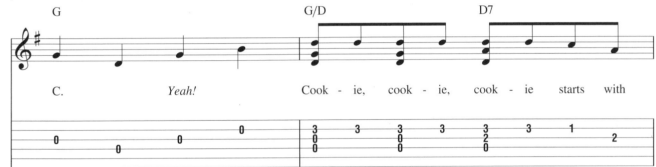

cook - ie, cook - ie, cook - ie starts with C. | 2. C. 3. *Hey, you know what?*

⊕ **Coda**

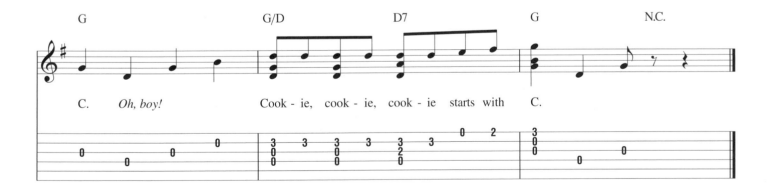

C. *Yeah!* Cook - ie, cook - ie, cook - ie starts with

C. *Oh, boy!* Cook - ie, cook - ie, cook - ie starts with C.

Additional Lyrics

3. *Hey, you know what?*
   A round cookie with one bite out of it looks like a C.
   A round doughnut with one bite out of it also looks like a C,
   But it is not as good as a cookie.
   Oh, and the moon sometimes looks like a C, but you can't eat that, so...

Candle on the Water

from Walt Disney's PETE'S DRAGON

Words and Music by Al Kasha and Joel Hirschhorn

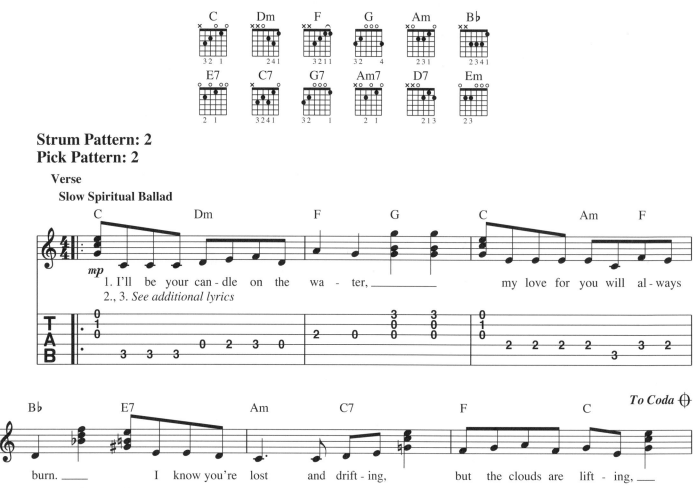

Strum Pattern: 2
Pick Pattern: 2

Verse
Slow Spiritual Ballad

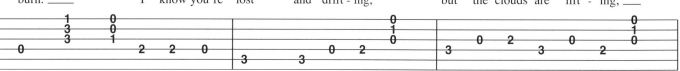

1. I'll be your can-dle on the wa-ter, _____ my love for you will al-ways
2., 3. *See additional lyrics*

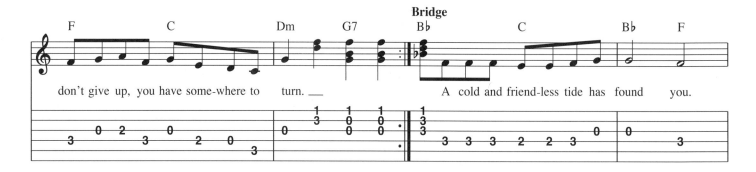

burn. _____ I know you're lost and drift-ing, but the clouds are lift-ing, ___

don't give up, you have some-where to turn. ___ A cold and friend-less tide has found you.

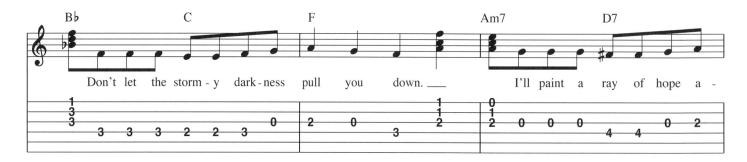

Don't let the storm-y dark-ness pull you down. ___ I'll paint a ray of hope a-

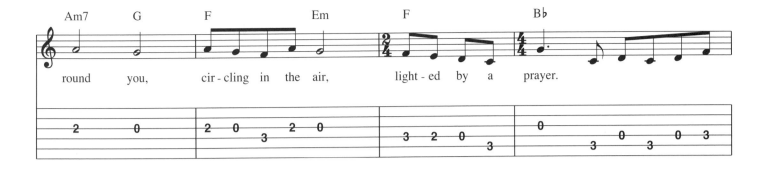

round you,   cir-cling in the air,   light-ed by a   prayer.

D.C. al Coda

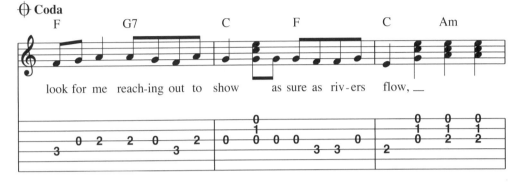

Coda

look for me reach-ing out to show   as sure as riv-ers flow, __

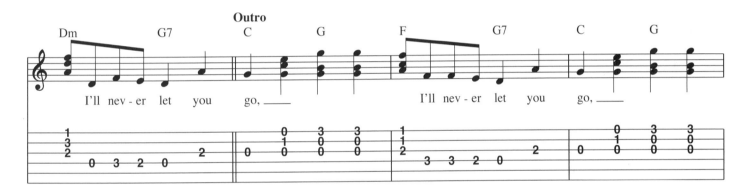

Outro

I'll nev-er let you go, _____   I'll nev-er let you go, _____

I'll nev-er let you go.

Additional Lyrics

2. I'll be your candle on the water,
   'Til ev'ry wave is warm and bright.
   My soul is there beside you,
   Let this candle guide you;
   Soon you'll see a golden stream of light.

3. I'll be your candle on the water,
   This flame inside of me will grow.
   Keep holding on, you'll make it,
   Here's my hand so take it;
   Look for me reaching out to show
   As sure as rivers flow,
   I'll never let you go,

Castle on a Cloud

from LES MISERABLES

Music by Claude-Michel Schönberg
Lyrics by Alain Boublil, Jean-Marc Natel and Herbert Kretzmer

*Strum Pattern: 7
*Pick Pattern: 7

*Use Pattern 4 for 4/4 measures.

Music and Lyrics Copyright © 1980 by Editions Musicales Alain Boublil
English Lyrics Copyright © 1986 by Alain Boublil Music Ltd., (ASCAP)
Mechanical and Publication Rights for the U.S.A. Administered by Alain Boublil Music Ltd. (ASCAP) c/o Joel Faden & Co., Inc.,
MLM 250 West 57th St., 26th Floor, New York, NY 10107, Tel. (212) 246-7203, Fax (212) 246-7217, mwlock@joelfaden.com

Additional Lyrics

2. There is a room that's full of toys.
   There are a hundred boys and girls.
   Nobody shouts or talks too loud,
   Not in my castle on a cloud.

3. I know a place where no one's lost.
   I know a place where no one cries.
   Crying at all is not allowed,
   Not in my castle on a cloud.

The Chicken Dance

By Terry Rendall and Werner Thomas
English Lyrics by Paul Parnes

Strum Pattern: 5
Pick Pattern: 1

Additional Lyrics

2. Hey, you're in the swing.
   You're cluckin' like a bird. (Pluck, pluck, pluck, pluck.)
   You're flappin' your wings.
   Don't you feel absurd. (No, no, no, no.)
   It's a chicken dance,
   Like a rooster an' a hen. (Ya, ya, ya, ya.)
   Flappy chicken dance;
   Let's do it again.

Chorus 2 Relax an' let the music move you.
   Let all your inhibitions go.
   Just watch your partner whirl around you.
   We're havin' fun now; I told you so.

3. Now you're flappin' like a bird
   And you're wigglin' too. (I like that move.)
   You're without a care.
   It's a dance for you. (Just made for you.)
   Keep doin' what you do.
   Don't you cop out now. (Don't cop out now.)
   Gets better as you dance;
   Catch your breath somehow.

4. Now we're almost through,
   Really flying high. (Bye, bye, bye, bye.)
   All you chickens and birds,
   Time to say goodbye. (To say goodbye.)
   Goin' back to the nest,
   But the flyin' was fun. (Oh, it was fun.)
   Chicken dance was the best,
   But the dance is done.

Chopsticks

By Arthur de Lulli

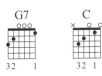

Strum Pattern: 8
Pick Pattern: 8

Intro
Fast

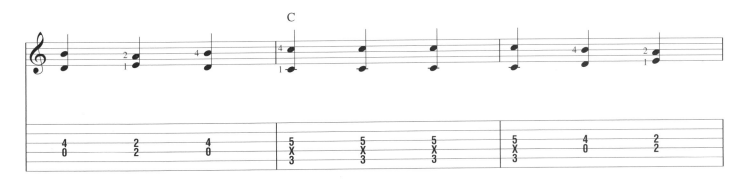

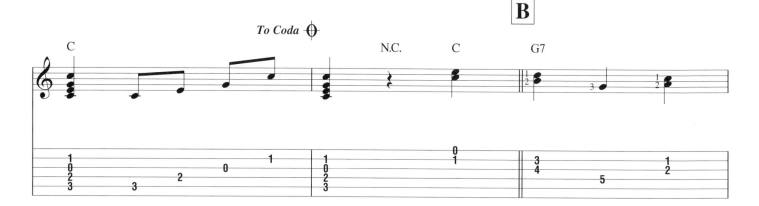

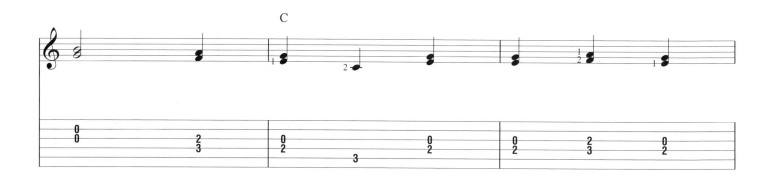

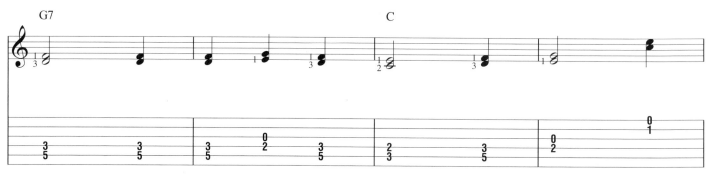

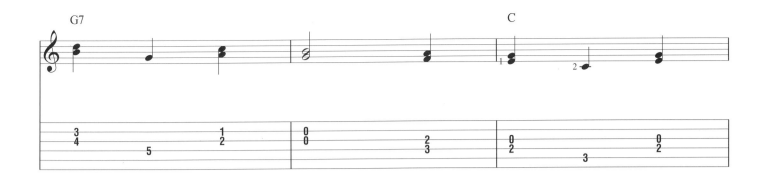

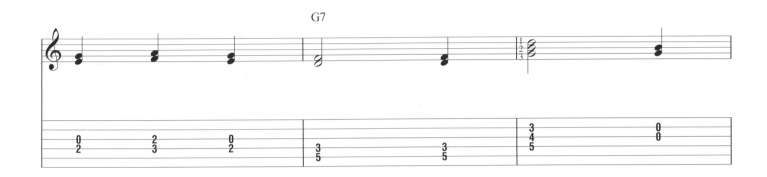

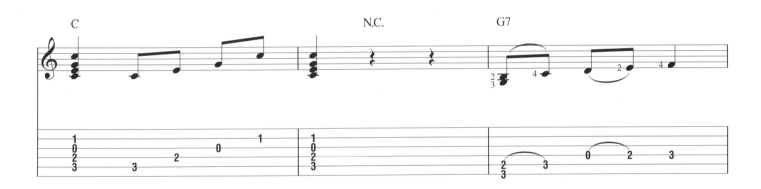

D.S. al Coda

 Coda

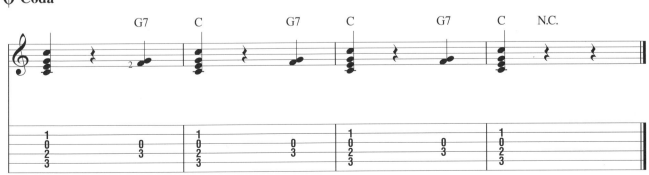

Chitty Chitty Bang Bang

Words and Music by Richard M. Sherman and Robert B. Sherman

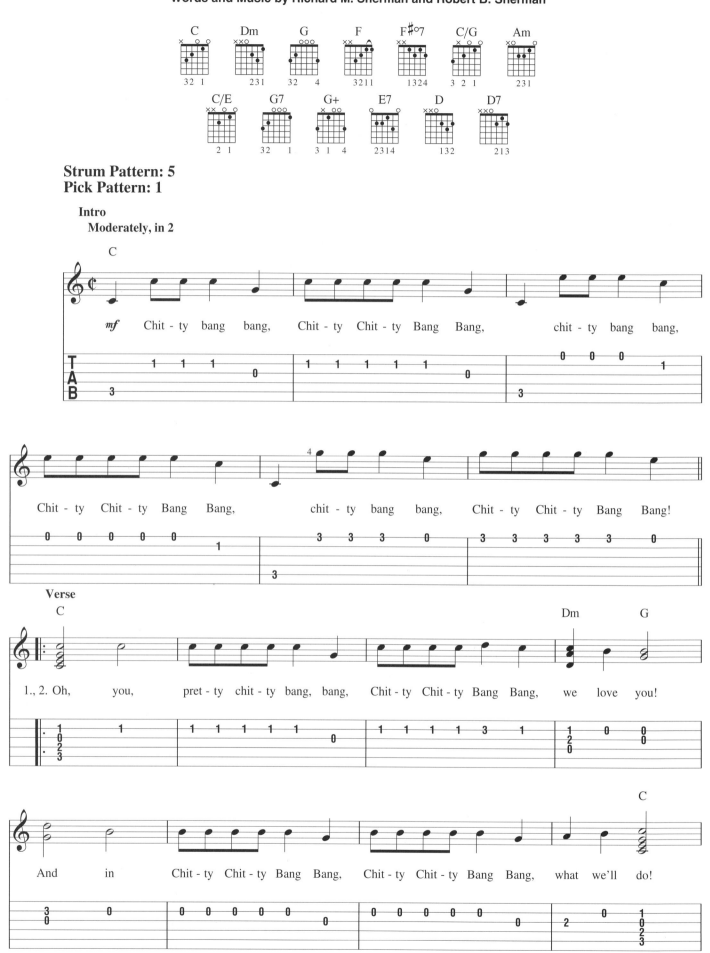

Bridge

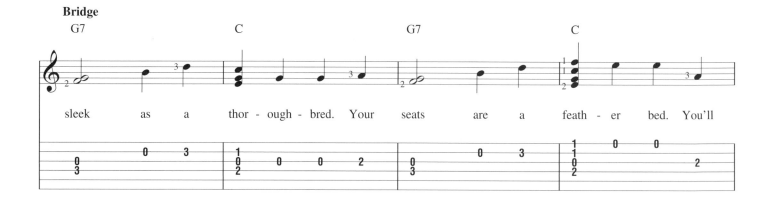

sleek   as   a   thor - ough - bred.   Your   seats   are   a   feath - er   bed.   You'll

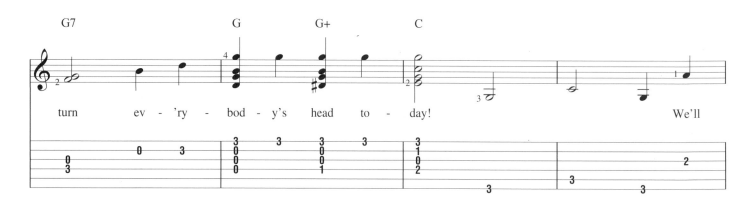

turn   ev - 'ry - bod - y's   head   to - day!   We'll

glide   on   our   mo - tor   trip,   with   pride   in   our   own - er - ship,   the

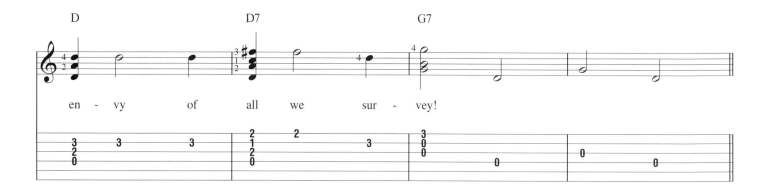

en - vy   of   all   we   sur - vey!

Verse

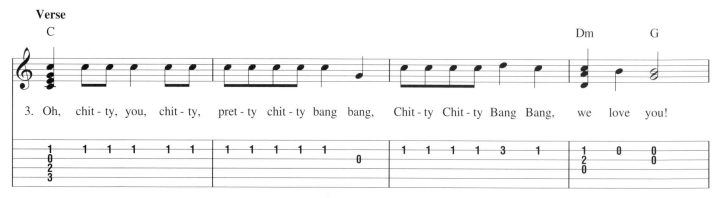

3. Oh,   chit - ty,   you,   chit - ty,   pret - ty   chit - ty   bang   bang,   Chit - ty   Chit - ty   Bang   Bang,   we   love   you!

(Oh, My Darling) Clementine

Words and Music by Percy Montrose

Strum Pattern: 9
Pick Pattern: 7

Verse
Moderately

1. In a cav - ern, in a can - yon, ex - ca - vat - ing for a mine, dwelt a min - er for - ty
2.-5. *See additional lyrics*

Chorus

nin - er and his daugh - ter, Clem-en-tine. Oh, my dar - ling, oh, my dar - ling, oh my dar - ling Clem-en-

tine, you are lost and gone for - ev - er, dread-ful sor - ry Clem - en - tine. __ 2. Light she tine. __

Additional Lyrics

2. Light she was and like a fairy
   And her shoes were number nine,
   Herring boxes without topses
   Sandals were for Clementine.

3. Drove she ducklings to the water
   Ev'ry morning just at nine,
   Stubbed her toe upon a splinter
   Fell into the foaming brine.

4. Ruby lips above the water
   Blowing bubbles soft and fine,
   But alas I was no swimmer
   So I lost my Clementine.

5. There's a churchyard on the hillside
   Where the flowers grow and twine,
   There grow roses 'mongst the posies
   Fertilized by Clementine.

Dites-Moi (Tell Me Why)

from SOUTH PACIFIC
Lyrics by Oscar Hammerstein II
Music by Richard Rodgers

Strum Pattern: 3
Pick Pattern: 1

Intro
Moderately

Verse

1., 2. Tell me why _____ the sky _____ is filled with mu - sic, _____ tell me why _____

_____ we fly _____ on clouds a - bove. _____ Can it be _____ that we _____ can fly to

mu - sic just be - cause, just be - cause we're ___ in ___ love? love? love?

French Lyrics

Dites-moi pourquoi la vie est belle,
Dites-moi pourquoi la vie est gai?
Dites-moi pourquoi, chère mad'moiselle,
Est-ce que parceque vous m'aimez?

Colors of the Wind

from Walt Disney's POCAHONTAS

Music by Alan Menken

Lyrics by Stephen Schwartz

Strum Pattern: 2
Pick Pattern: 2

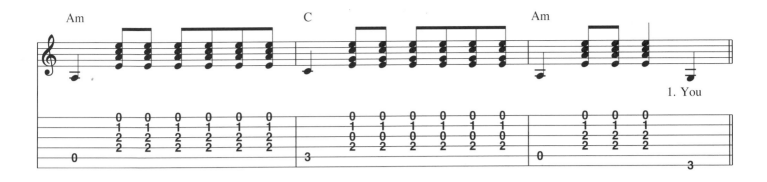

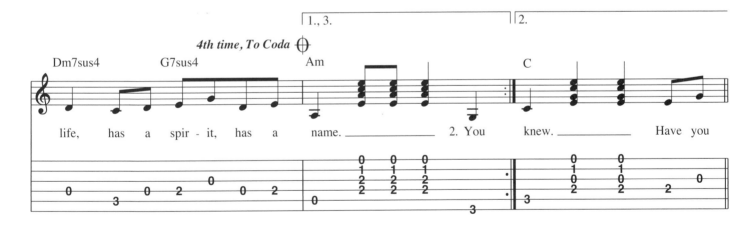

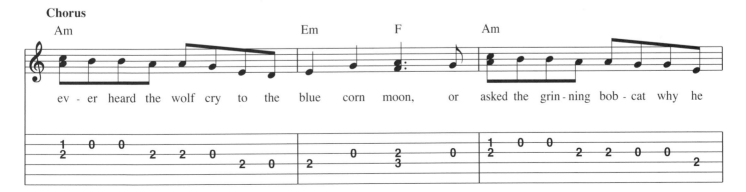

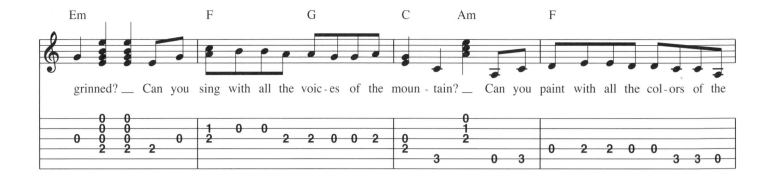

grinned? __ Can you sing with all the voic - es of the moun - tain? __ Can you paint with all the col - ors of the

D.S. al Coda

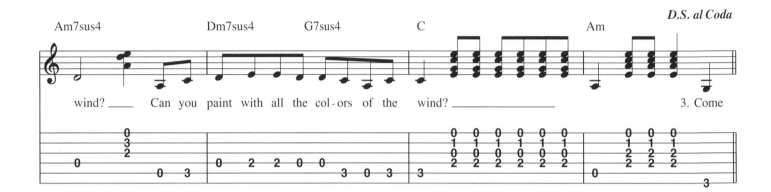

wind? _____ Can you paint with all the col - ors of the wind? _____ 3. Come

Coda

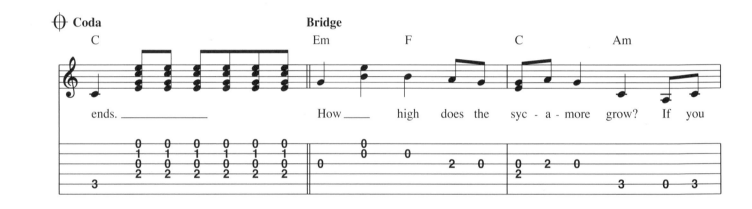

ends. _____ How _____ high does the syc - a - more grow? If you

Bridge

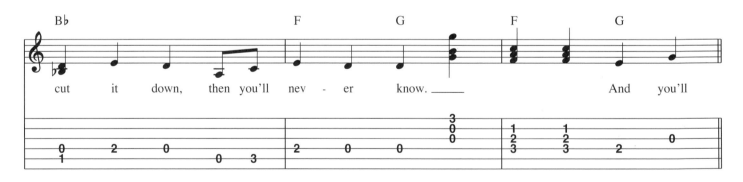

cut it down, then you'll nev - er know. _____ And you'll

Chorus

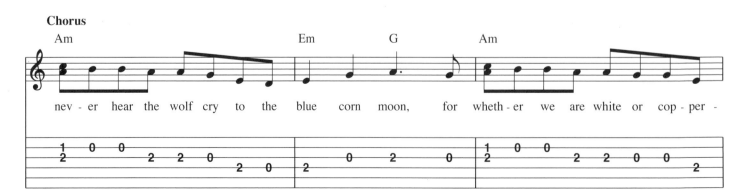

nev - er hear the wolf cry to the blue corn moon, for wheth - er we are white or cop - per -

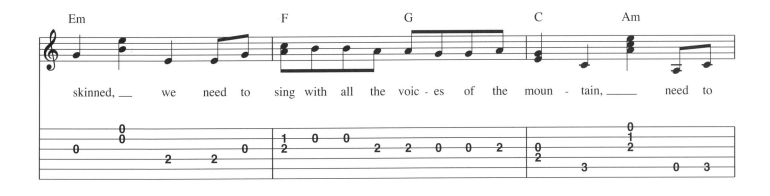

skinned, __ we need to sing with all the voic - es of the moun - tain, _____ need to

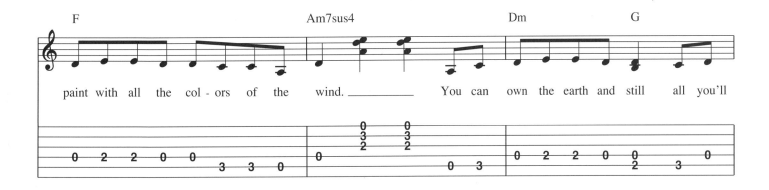

paint with all the col - ors of the wind. _____ You can own the earth and still all you'll

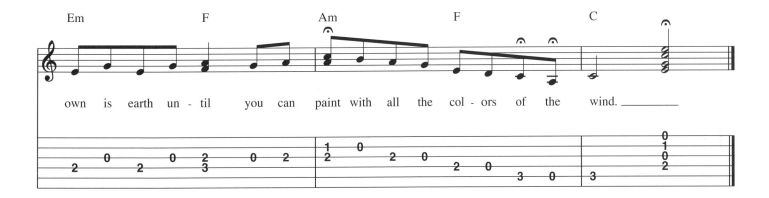

own is earth un - til you can paint with all the col - ors of the wind. _____

Additional Lyrics

2. You think the only people who are people
   Are the people who look and think like you,
   But if you walk the footsteps of a stranger
   You'll learn things you never knew you never knew.

3. Come run the hidden pine trails of the forest,
   Come taste the sunsweet berries of the earth;
   Come roll in all the riches all around you,
   And for once never wonder what they're worth.

4. The rainstorm and the river are my brothers;
   The heron and the otter are my friends;
   And we are all connected to each other
   In a circle, in a hoop that never ends.

Consider Yourself

from the Broadway Musical OLIVER!

Words and Music by Lionel Bart

Day-O
(The Banana Boat Song)

Words and Music by Irving Burgie and William Attaway

wan' go home. Stack ba - nan - a till de morn - ing come.

Verse

Day-light come __ and me wan' go home. 2. Come, mis-ter tal-ly man, tal-ly me ba-nan - a.

Day - light come __ and me wan' go home. Come, mis-ter tal - ly man,

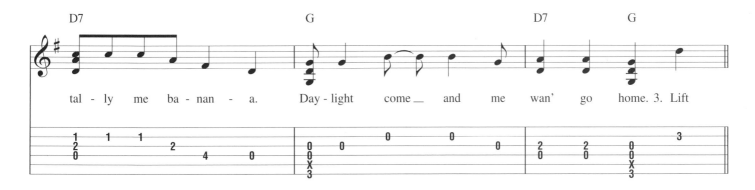

tal - ly me ba-nan - a. Day-light come __ and me wan' go home. 3. Lift

𝄋 Verse

G

(6.) six foot, sev-en foot, eight foot bunch. Day-light come __ and me

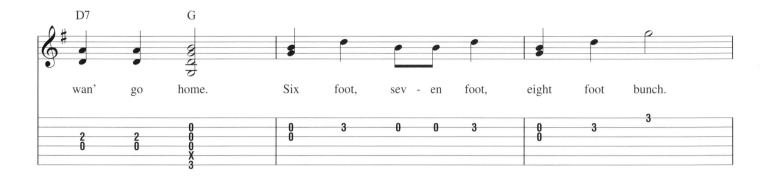

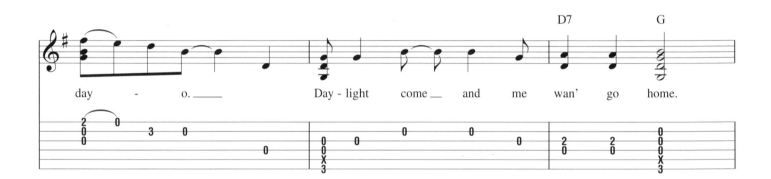

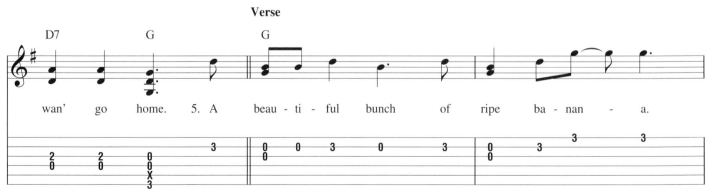

Day - light come __ and me wan' go home.   Hide the dead - ly

D.S. al Coda

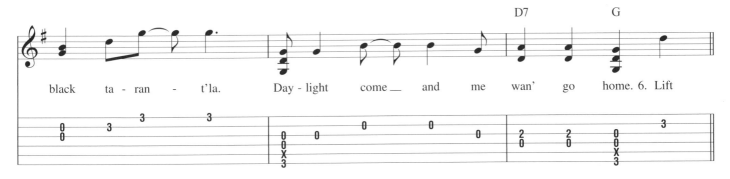

black ta - ran - t'la.   Day - light come __ and me wan' go home. 6. Lift

⊕ Coda   **Verse**

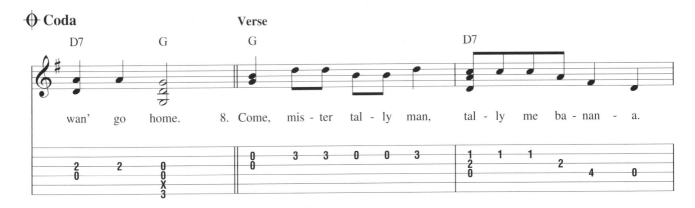

wan' go home.   8. Come, mis - ter tal - ly man,   tal - ly me ba - nan - a.

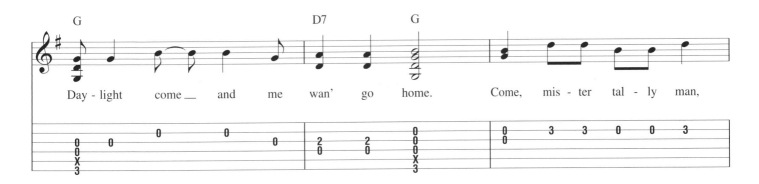

Day - light come __ and me wan' go home.   Come, mis - ter tal - ly man,

D.C. al Fine

tal - ly me ba - nan - a.   Day - light come __ and me wan' go home.

Ding-Dong! The Witch Is Dead

from THE WIZARD OF OZ

Lyric by E.Y. "Yip" Harburg
Music by Harold Arlen

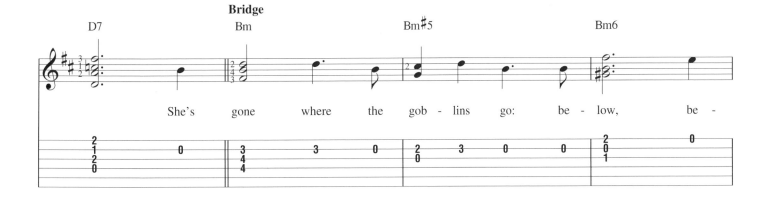

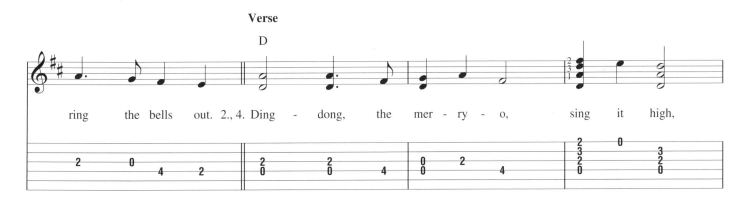

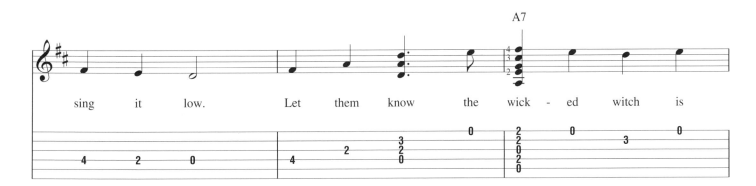

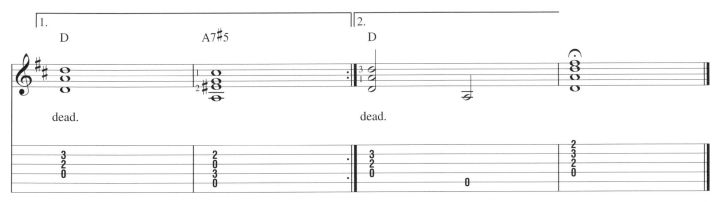

For He's a Jolly Good Fellow

Traditional

Strum Pattern: 7, 8
Pick Pattern: 8

no - bod - y can de - ny! _____ Which

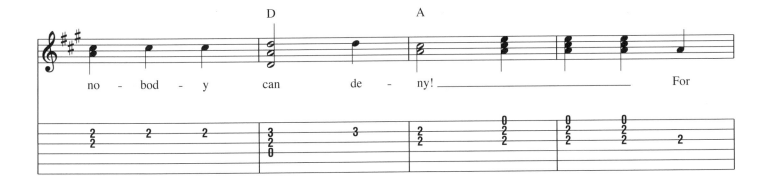

no - bod - y can de - ny! _____ For

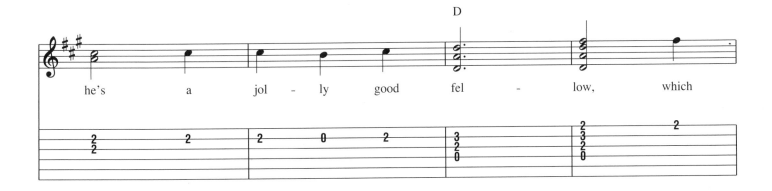

he's a jol - ly good fel - low, which

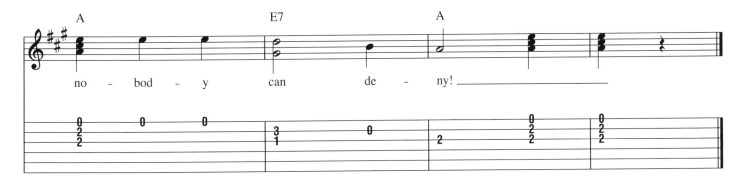

no - bod - y can de - ny! _____

Friend Like Me

from Walt Disney's ALADDIN

Lyrics by Howard Ashman
Music by Alan Menken

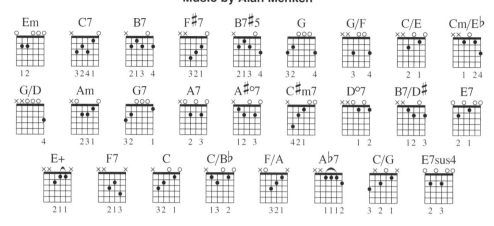

Strum Pattern: 5
Pick Pattern: 1

Intro
Moderately slow, in 2

1. Well, A - li

Verse

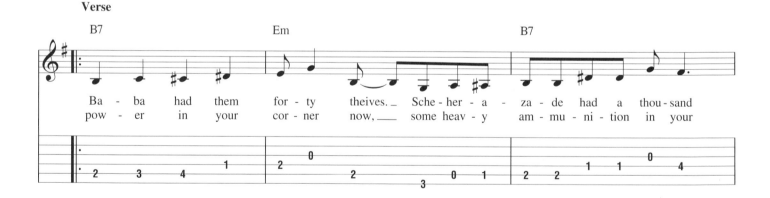

Ba - ba had them for - ty thei ves.__ Sche - her - a - za - de had a thou - sand
pow - er in your cor - ner now,__ some heav - y am - mu - ni - tion in your

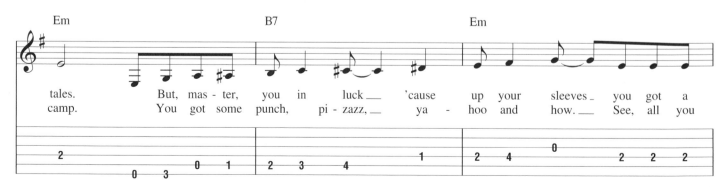

tales.   But, mas - ter, you in luck __ 'cause up your sleeves __ you got a
camp.   You got some punch, pi - zazz, __ ya - hoo and how. __ See, all you

ab - ra - ca - da - bra, let 'er rip and then make the suck-er dis-ap - pear? 3. So don't ya

Verse

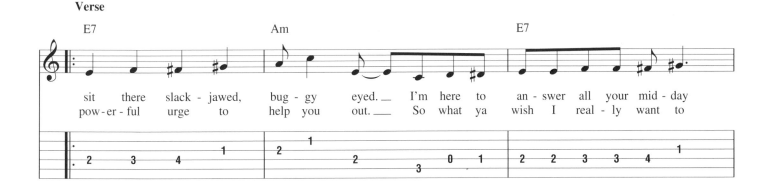

sit there slack - jawed, bug - gy eyed. __ I'm here to an - swer all your mid - day
pow-er - ful urge to help you out. __ So what ya wish I real - ly want to

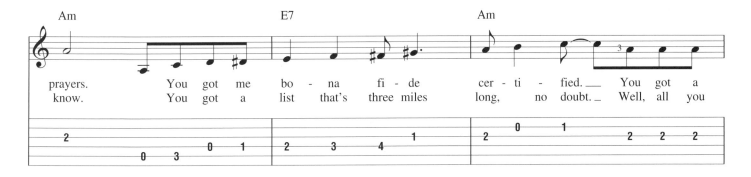

prayers. You got me bo - na fi - de cer - ti - fied. __ You got a
know. You got a list that's three miles long, no doubt. __ Well, all you

ge - nie for your chargé d'af - faires. 4. I got a so. And oh, _____
got - ta do is rub like

Outro-Chorus

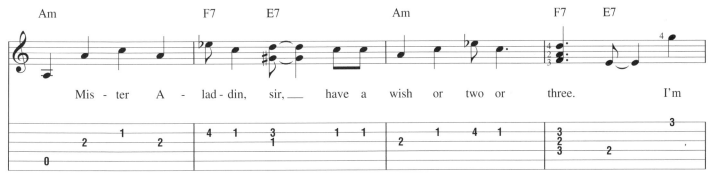

Mis - ter A - lad-din, sir, __ have a wish or two or three. I'm

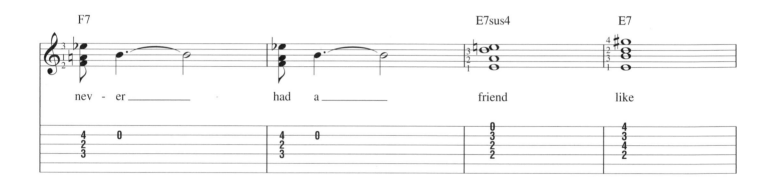

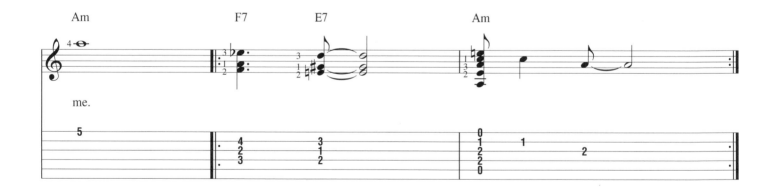

Hail, Hail, the Gang's All Here

Words by D.A. Esrom
Music by Theodore F. Morse and Arthur Sullivan

Strum Pattern: 7, 8
Pick Pattern: 7, 8

Moderately

Getting to Know You

from THE KING AND I

Lyrics by Oscar Hammerstein II
Music by Richard Rodgers

Give a Little Whistle

Words by Ned Washington
Music by Leigh Harline

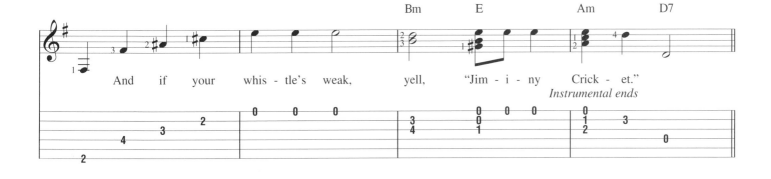

And if your whis-tle's weak, yell, "Jim-i-ny Crick-et."

Instrumental ends

Verse

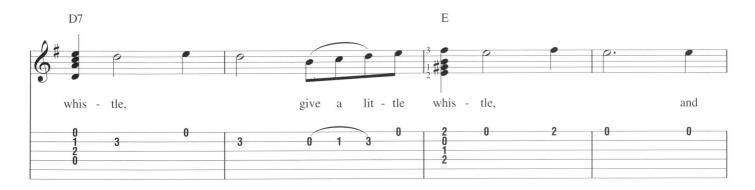

3., 6. Take the straight and nar-row path and if you start to slide, give a lit-tle

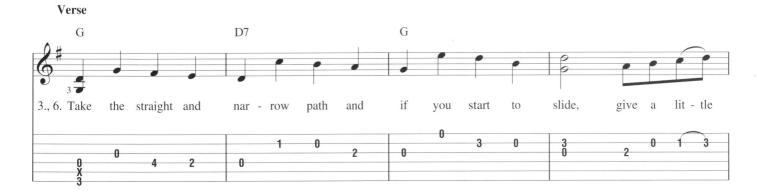

whis-tle, give a lit-tle whis-tle, and

To Coda ⊕   *D.C. al Coda*
(take repeat)

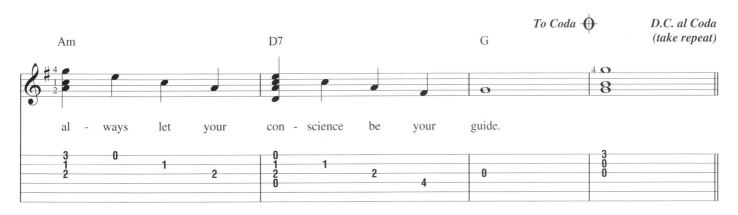

al - ways let your con - science be your guide.

⊕ Coda

And al - ways let your con - science be your guide.

Grandfather's Clock

By Henry Clay Work

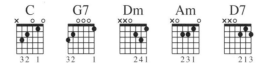

Strum Pattern: 3
Pick Pattern: 3

Verse
Moderately slow

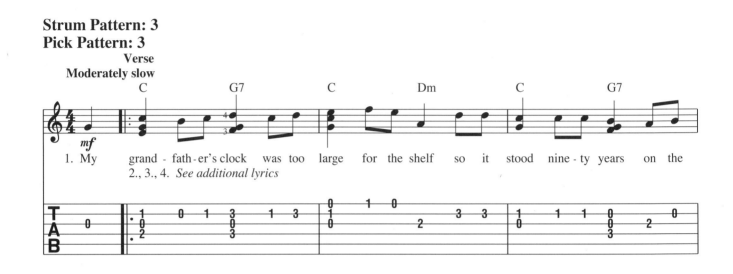

1. My grand - fath - er's clock was too large for the shelf so it stood nine - ty years on the
2., 3., 4. *See additional lyrics*

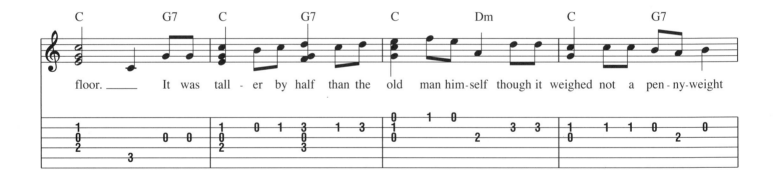

floor. _____ It was tall - er by half than the old man him-self though it weighed not a pen - ny-weight

more. _____ It was bought on the morn of the day that he was born and was al - ways his trea - sure and

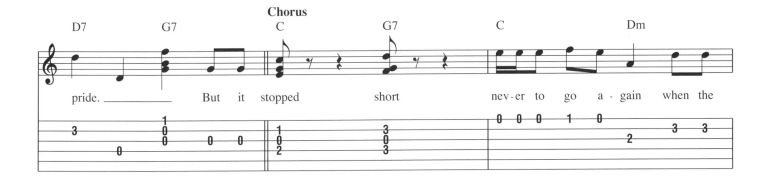

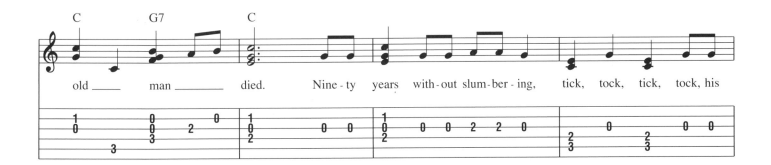

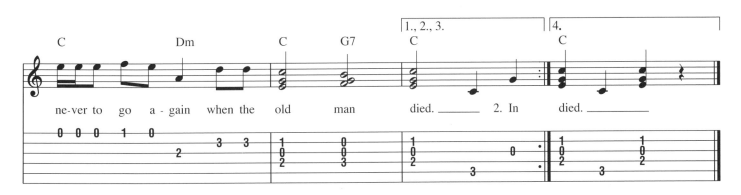

Additional Lyrics

2. In watching its pendulum swing to and fro,
   Many hours had he spent while a boy;
   And in childhood and manhood the clock seemed to know,
   And to share both his grief and his joy.
   For it struck twenty-four when he entered at the door,
   With a blooming and beautiful bride.

3. My grandfather said that of those he could hire,
   Not a servant so faithful he found;
   For it wasted no time, and had but one desire,
   At the close of each week to be wound.
   And it kept in its place, not a frown upon its face,
   And its hands never hung by its side.

4. It rang an alarm in the dead of the night,
   An alarm that for years had been dumb;
   And we knew that his spirit was pluming its flight,
   That his hour of departure had come.
   Still the clock kept the time, with a soft and muffled chime,
   As we silently stood by his side.

Hakuna Matata

from Walt Disney Pictures' THE LION KING

Music by Elton John
Lyrics by Tim Rice

Verse

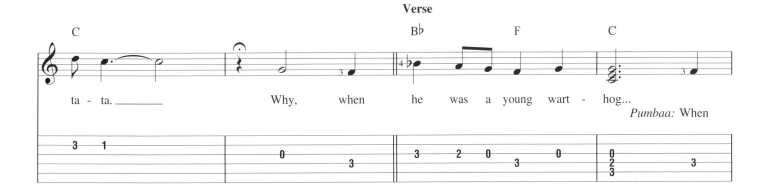

65

shame!
Thought of chang-ing my name, *Oh, what's in a name?* and I got down - heart - ed _____ *How did you*

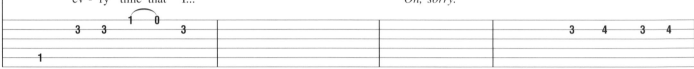

feel?
ev -'ry time that I... *Hey, Pumbaa, not in front of the kids.* *Oh, sorry.* *Timon & Pumbaa:* Ha - ku - na ma -

Chorus

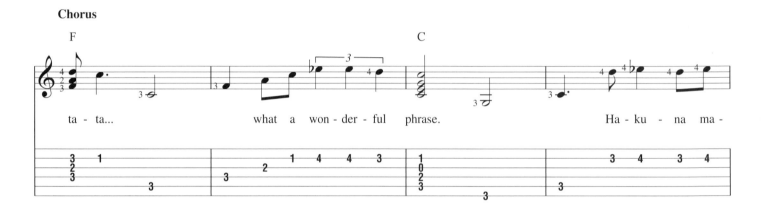

ta - ta... what a won - der - ful phrase. Ha - ku - na ma -

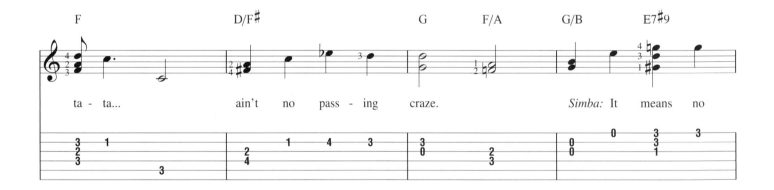

ta - ta... ain't no pass - ing craze. *Simba:* It means no

wor - ries for the rest ___ of your days. *All:* It's our

Interlude

Outro

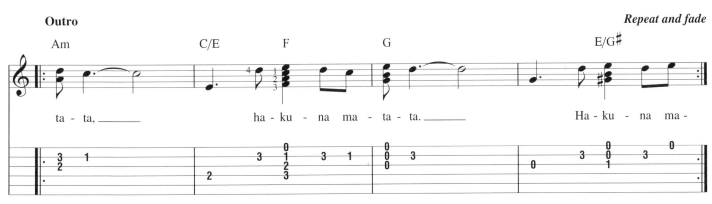

Happy Birthday to You

Words and Music by Mildred J. Hill and Patty S. Hill

He's Got the Whole World in His Hands

Traditional Spiritual

Strum Pattern: 3, 4
Pick Pattern: 1, 3

Additional Lyrics

2. He's got the wind and the rain in His hands,
   He's got the wind and the rain in His hands,
   He's got the wind and the rain in His hands,
   He's got the whole world in His hands.

3. He's got the tiny little baby in His hands,
   He's got the tiny little baby in His hands,
   He's got the tiny little baby in His hands,
   He's got the whole world in His hands.

4. He's got you and me, brother, in his hands,
   He's got you and me, sister, in his hands,
   He's got you and me, brother, in his hands,
   He's got the whole world sin his hands.

Heart and Soul

Words by Frank Loesser
Music by Hoagy Carmichael

thrill - ing. Nev - er be - fore were mine so strange - ly

Verse

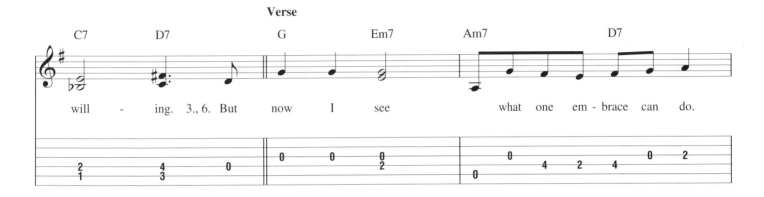

will - ing. 3., 6. But now I see what one em - brace can do.

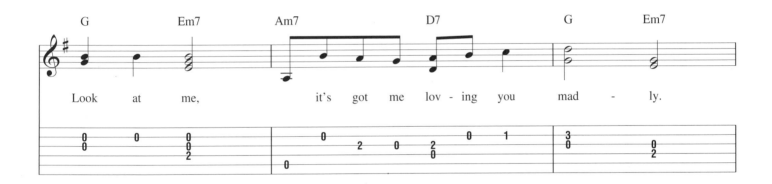

Look at me, it's got me lov - ing you mad - ly.

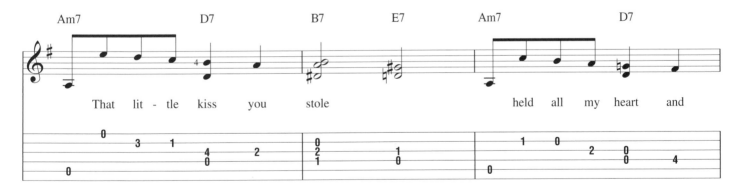

That lit - tle kiss you stole held all my heart and

To Coda ⊕   *D.C. al Coda*
                     (take repeat)   ⊕ **Coda**

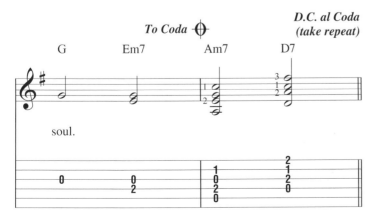

soul.

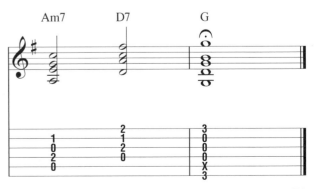

Hi-Lili, Hi-Lo

Words by Helen Deutsch
Music by Bronislau Kaper

Strum Pattern: 8
Pick Pattern: 8

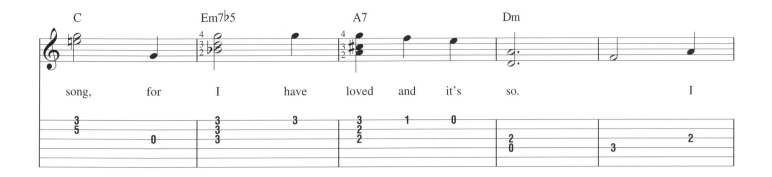

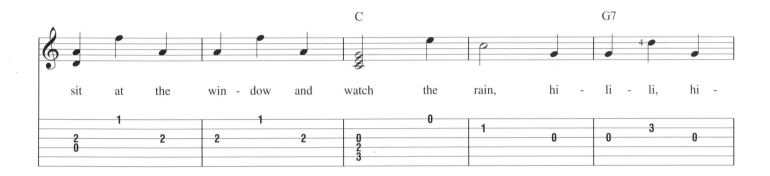

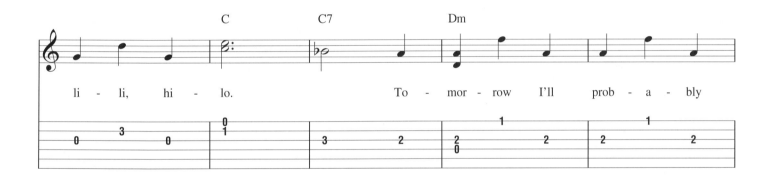

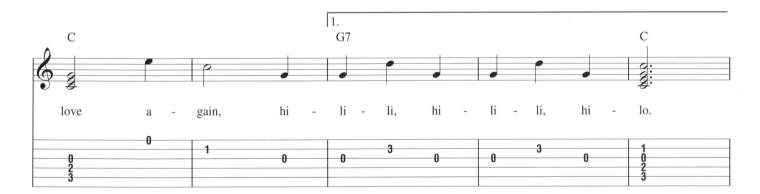

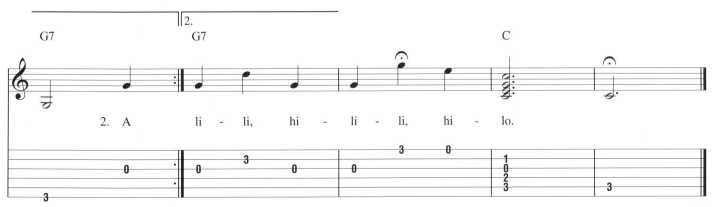

The Hokey Pokey

Words and Music by Charles P. Macak, Tafft Baker and Larry LaPrise

Strum Pattern: 6
Pick Pattern: 6

1. You put your right foot in, ___ you put your right foot out. ___ You put your
2. - 10. *See additional lyrics*

right foot in, ___ and you shake it all a-bout. You do the Hok-ey Pok-ey, and you

turn your-self a-round. That's what it's all a-bout. 2. You put your bout.

Additional Lyrics

2. You put your left foot in...

3. You put your right arm in...

4. You put your left arm in...

5. You put your right elbow in...

6. You put your left elbow in...

7. You put your head in...

8. You put your right hip in...

9. You put your left hip in...

10. You put your whole self in...

I Enjoy Being a Girl

from FLOWER DRUM SONG
Lyrics by Oscar Hammerstein II
Music by Richard Rodgers

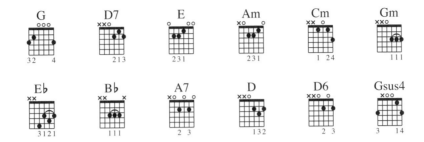

Strum Pattern: 2, 5
Pick Pattern: 1, 3

Bridge

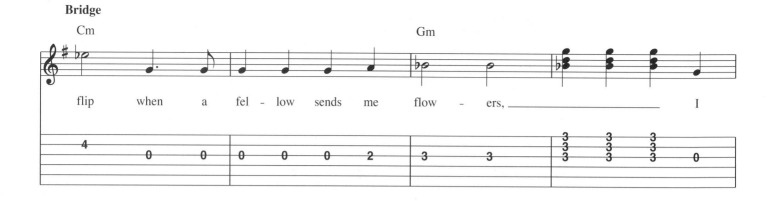

flip when a fel - low sends me flow - ers, _____ I

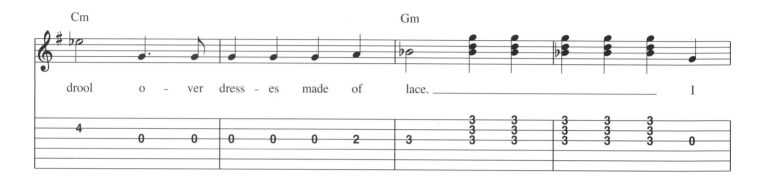

drool o - ver dress - es made of lace. _____ I

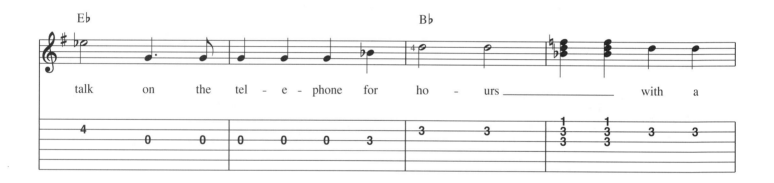

talk on the tel - e - phone for ho - urs _____ with a

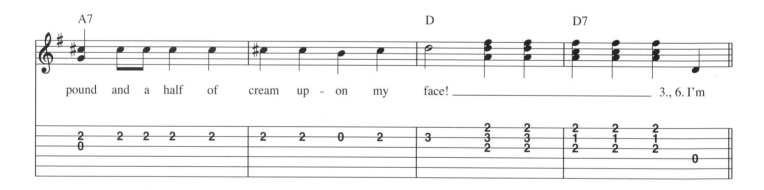

pound and a half of cream up - on my face! _____ 3., 6. I'm

Verse

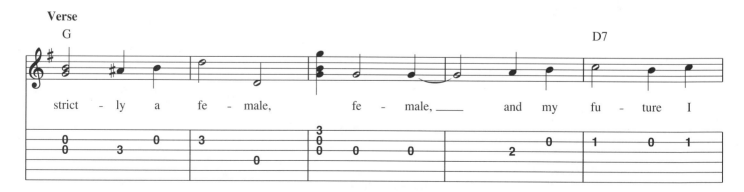

strict - ly a fe - male, fe - male, _____ and my fu - ture I

hope will be _____ in the home of a brave and

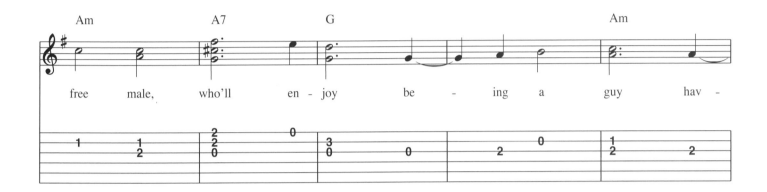

free male, who'll en - joy be - ing a guy hav -

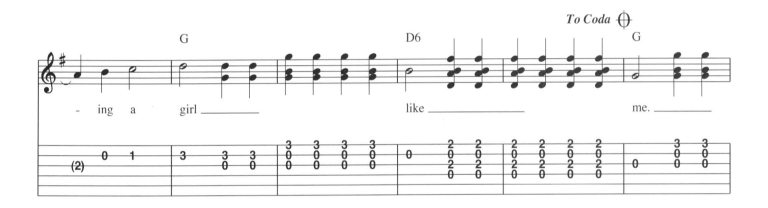

- ing a girl _____ like _____ me. _____

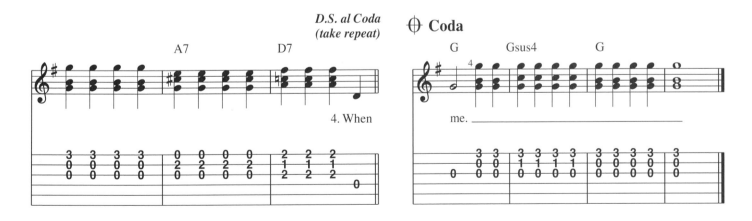

4. When

me. _____

Additional Lyrics

2., 5. When men say I'm cute and funny
And my teeth aren't teeth but pearl,
I just lap it up like honey,
I enjoy being a girl!

How Much Is That Doggie in the Window

Words and Music by Bob Merrill

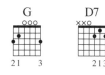

Strum Pattern: 7
Pick Pattern: 7

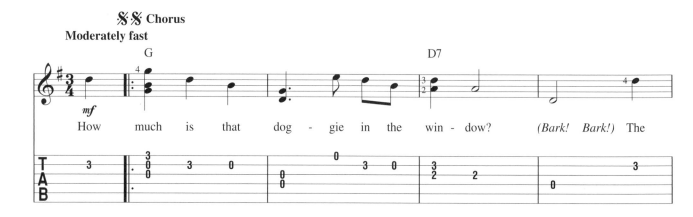

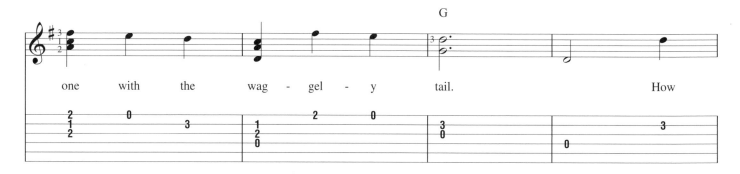

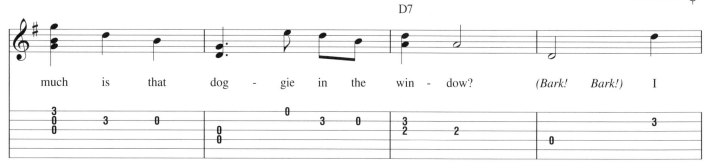

𝄋 **Verse**

To Coda 1 𝄌 | 1. | 2. | *D.S. al Coda 1*

𝄌 **Coda 1** *D.S.S. al Coda 2*   𝄌 **Coda 2**

The Hucklebuck

Lyrics by Roy Alfred
Music by Andy Gibson

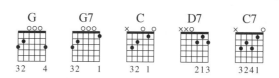

Strum Pattern: 3
Pick Pattern: 3

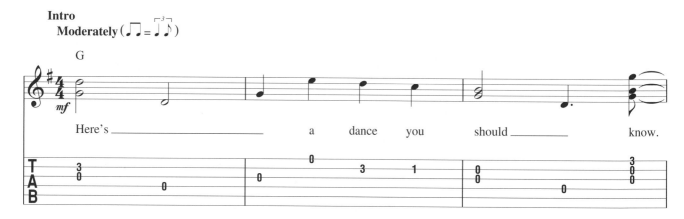

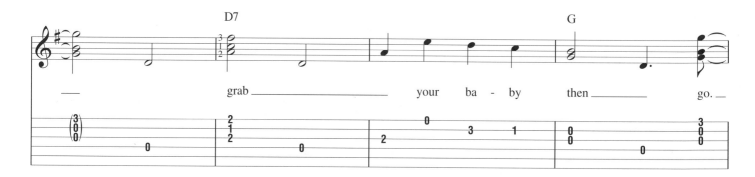

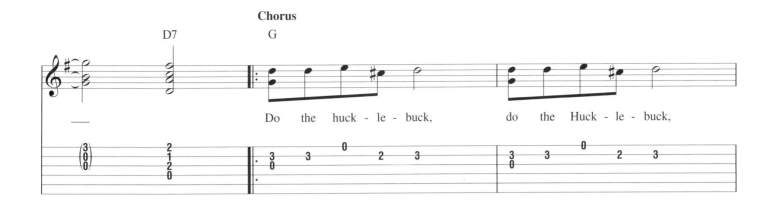

Chorus

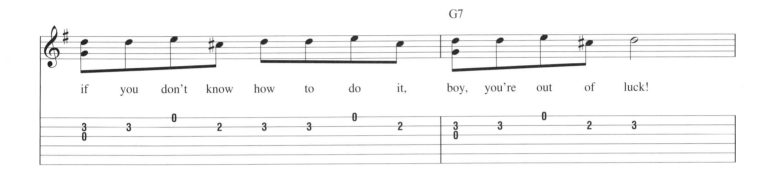

Do the huck - le - buck, do the Huck - le - buck,

if you don't know how to do it, boy, you're out of luck!

Push your part - ner out, then you hunch your back, start a lit - tle move - ment in your

sac - ro - il - i - ac. Wig - gle like a snake, wad - dle like a duck.

That's the way you do it when you do the Huck - le - buck. do the Huck - le - buck.

I Gave My Love a Cherry
(The Riddle Song)
Traditional

Strum Pattern: 2
Pick Pattern: 2

Additional Lyrics

2. How can there be a cherry that has no stone?
How can there be a chicken that has no bone?
How can there be a story that has no end?
How can there be a baby with no cryin'?

3. A cherry, when it's blooming, it has no stone.
A chicken, when it's pipping, it has no bone.
The story that I love, it has no end.
A baby, when it's sleeping, has no cryin'.

If I Only Had a Brain

from THE WIZARD OF OZ

Lyric by E.Y. "Yip" Harburg
Music by Harold Arlen

Strum Pattern: 3
Pick Pattern: 3

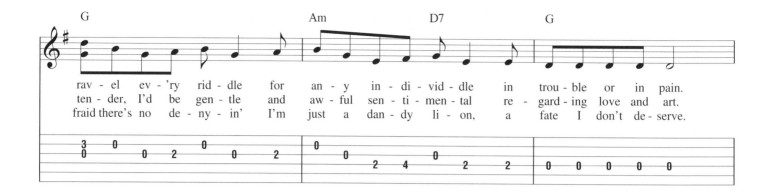

rav - el ev - 'ry rid - dle for an - y in - di - vid - dle in trou - ble or in pain.
ten - der, I'd be gen - tle and aw - ful sen - ti - men - tal re - gard - ing love and art.
fraid there's no de - ny - in' I'm just a dan - dy li - on, a fate I don't de - serve.

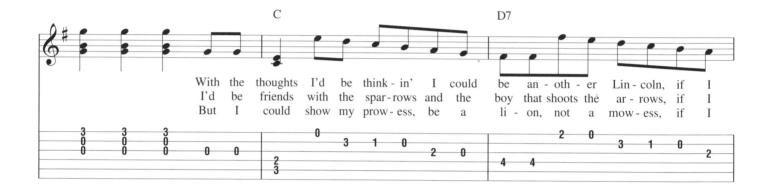

With the thoughts I'd be think - in' I could be an - oth - er Lin - coln, if I
I'd be friends with the spar - rows and the boy that shoots the ar - rows, if I
But I could show my prow - ess, be a li - on, not a mow - ess, if I

Bridge

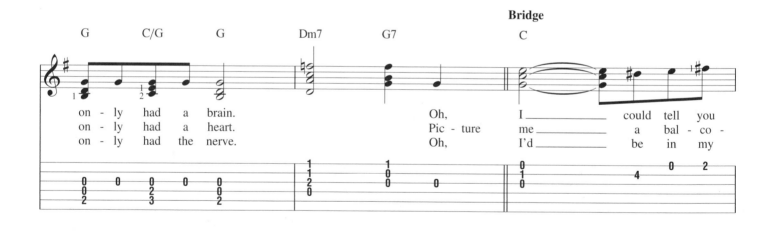

on - ly had a brain. Oh, I could tell you
on - ly had a heart. Pic - ture me a bal - co -
on - ly had the nerve. Oh, I'd be in my

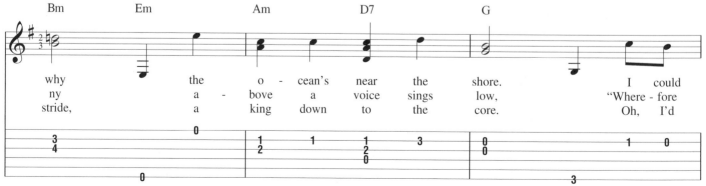

why the o - cean's near the shore. I could
ny a - bove a voice sings low, "Where - fore
stride, a king down to the core. Oh, I'd

84

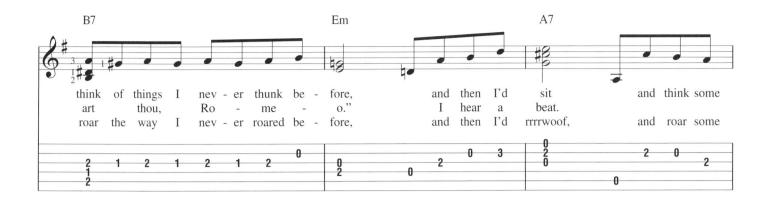

think of things I nev - er thunk be - fore,
art thou, Ro - me - o."
roar the way I nev - er roared be - fore,

and then I'd sit
I hear a beat.
and then I'd rrrrwoof,

and think some
and roar some

Verse

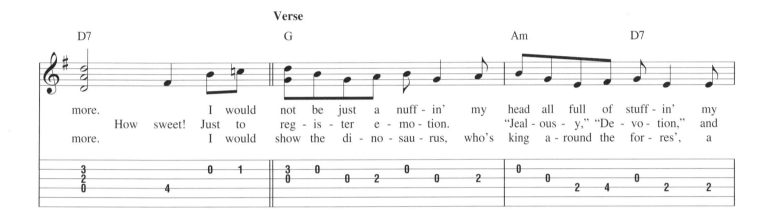

more. How sweet! Just to
How sweet! Just to
more. I would

I would not be just a nuff - in' my head all full of stuff - in' my
reg - is - ter e - mo - tion. "Jeal - ous - y," "De - vo - tion," and
show the di - no - sau - rus, who's king a - round the for - res', a

heart all full of pain.
real - ly feel the part,
king they bet - ter serve.

And per - haps I'd de - serve you and be
I would stay young and chip - per and I'd
Why, with my re - gal beez - er, I could

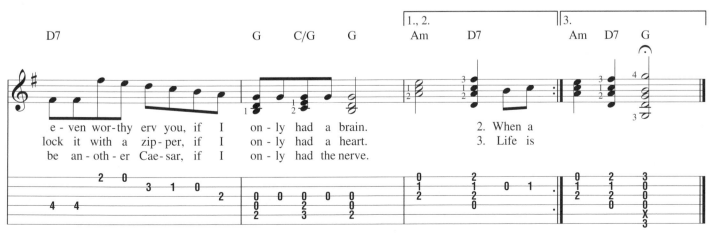

e - ven wor - thy erv you, if I
lock it with a zip - per, if I
be an - oth - er Cae - sar, if I

on - ly had a brain.
on - ly had a heart.
on - ly had the nerve.

2. When a
3. Life is

(I Scream - You Scream - We All Scream For)
Ice Cream

Words and Music by Howard Johnson, Billy Moll and Robert King

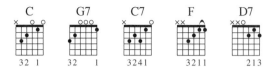

Strum Pattern: 4
Pick Pattern: 4

Verse
Moderately, in 2

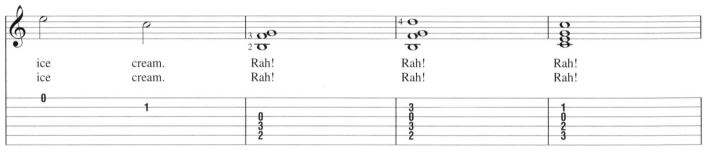

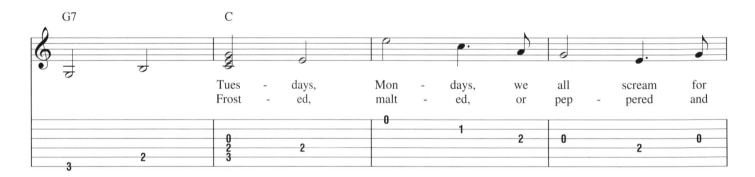

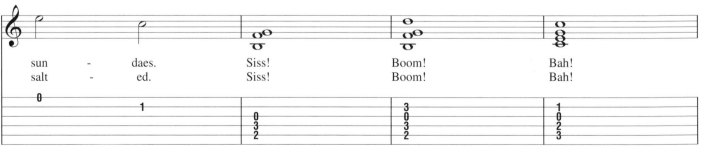

Bridge

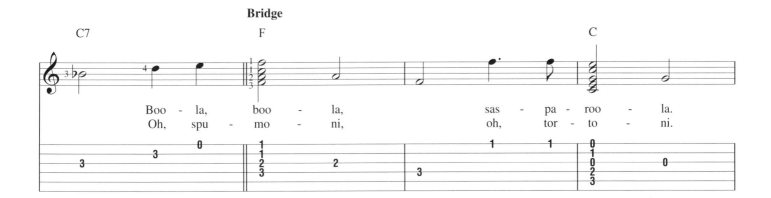

Boo - la, boo - la, sas - pa - roo - la.
Oh, spu - mo - ni, oh, tor - to - ni.

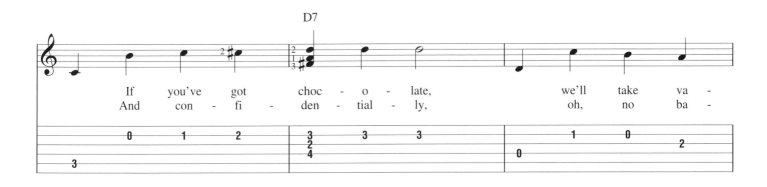

If you've got choc - o - late, we'll take va -
And con - fi - den - tial - ly, oh, no ba -

Verse

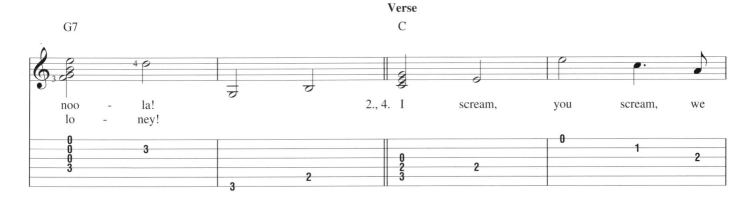

noo - la!
lo - ney!   2., 4. I scream, you scream, we

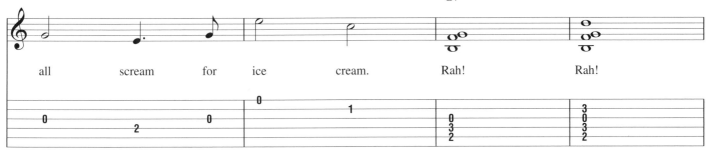

all scream for ice cream. Rah! Rah!

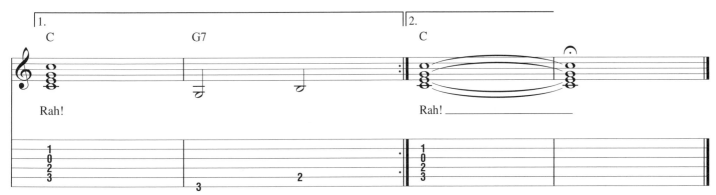

Rah!   Rah! _____

I Whistle a Happy Tune

from THE KING AND I

Lyrics by Oscar Hammerstein II
Music by Richard Rodgers

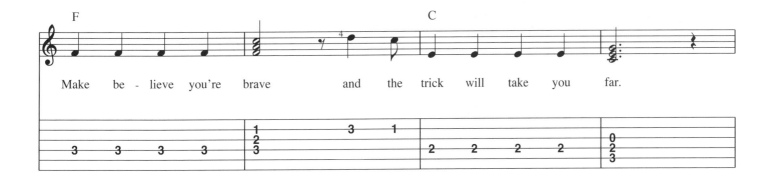

Make be - lieve you're brave and the trick will take you far.

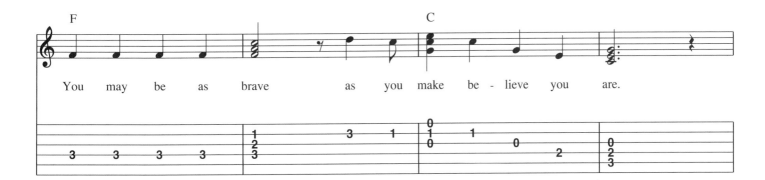

You may be as brave as you make be - lieve you are.

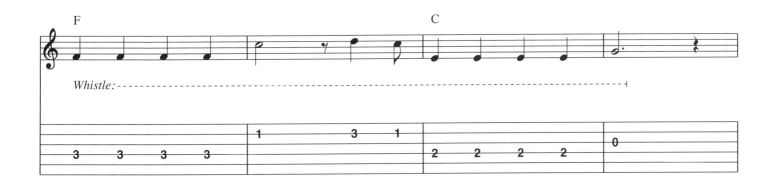

Whistle: -

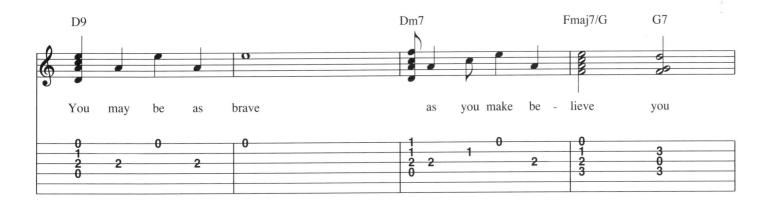

You may be as brave as you make be - lieve you

are.

I'd Like to Teach the World to Sing

Words and Music by Bill Backer, Roquel Davis, Roger Cook and Roger Greenaway

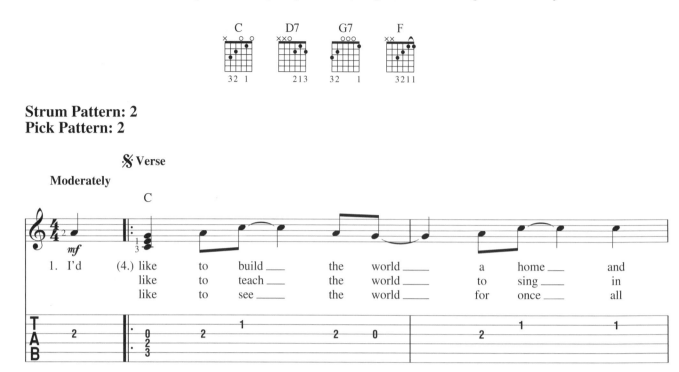

Strum Pattern: 2
Pick Pattern: 2

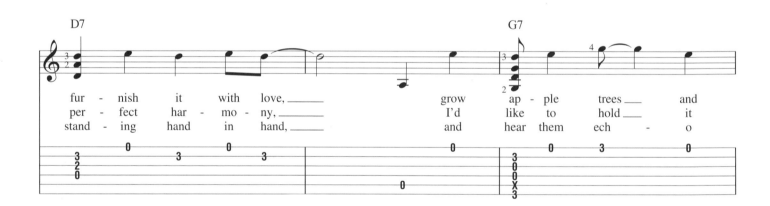

1. I'd (4.) like to build the world a home and
like to teach the world to sing in
like to see the world for once all

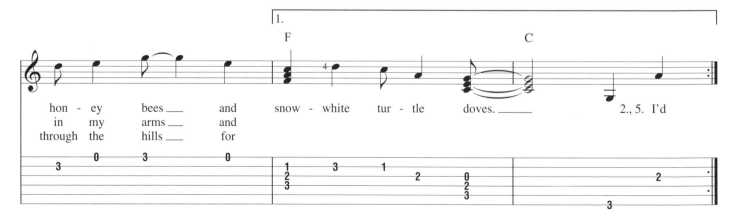

fur - nish it with love, grow ap - ple trees and
per - fect har - mo - ny, I'd like to hold it
stand - ing hand in hand, and hear them ech - o

hon - ey bees and snow - white tur - tle doves. 2., 5. I'd
in my arms and
through the hills for

I'm an Old Cowhand
(From the Rio Grande)

Words and Music by Johnny Mercer

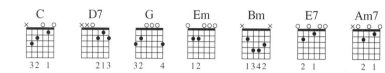

Strum Pattern: 3
Pick Pattern: 3

Verse

Moderately slow, in 2

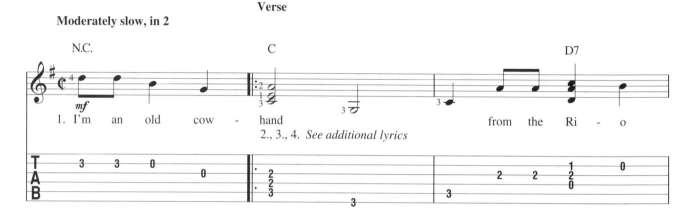

1. I'm an old cow-hand   from the Ri - o

2., 3., 4. *See additional lyrics*

Grande,   but my legs ain't bowed

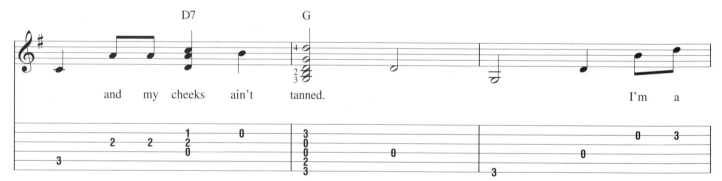

and my cheeks ain't tanned.   I'm a

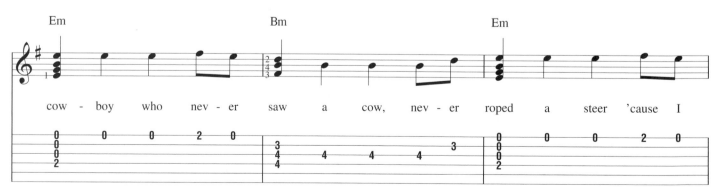

cow - boy who nev - er saw a cow, nev - er roped a steer 'cause I

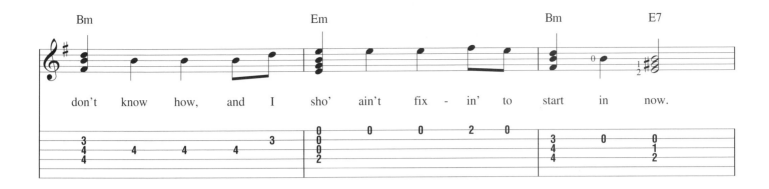

don't know how, and I sho' ain't fix - in' to start in now.

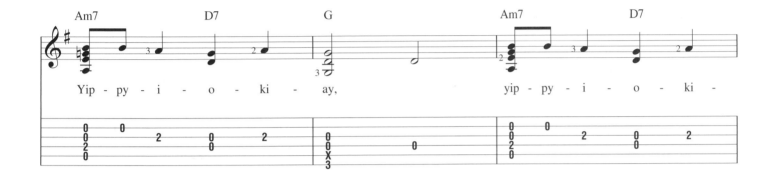

Yip - py - i - o - ki - ay, yip - py - i - o - ki -

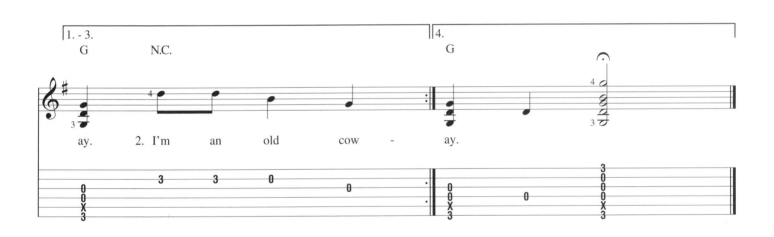

ay. 2. I'm an old cow - ay.

Additional Lyrics

2. I'm an old cowhand from the Rio Grande,
   And I learned to ride 'fore I learned to stand.
   I'm a ridin' fool who is up to date.
   I know ev'ry trail in the Lone Star State
   'Cause I ride the range in a Ford V8.
   Yippy-i-o-ki-ay, yippy-i-o-ki-ay.

3. I'm an old cowhand from the Rio Grande,
   And I come to town just to hear the band.
   I know all the songs that the cowboys know
   'Bout the big corral where the dogies go
   'Cause I learned them all on the radio.
   Yippy-i-o-ki-ay, yippy-i-o-ki-ay.

4. I'm an old cowhand from the Rio Grande,
   Where the West is wild 'round the Borderland,
   Where the buffalo roam around the zoo
   And the Indians make you a rug or two
   And the old Bar X is a Barbecue.
   Yippy-i-o-ki-ay, yippy-i-o-ki-ay.

I've Been Working on the Railroad

American Folksong

If You're Happy and You Know It

Words and Music by L. Smith

Strum Pattern: 1, 4
Pick Pattern: 2, 5

Additional Lyrics

2. If you're happy and you know it, stomp your feet. (stomp, stomp)
If you're happy and you know it, stomp your feet. (stomp, stomp)
If you're happy and you know it, then your face will surely show it.
If you're happy and you know it, stomp your feet. (stomp, stomp)

3. If you're happy and you know it, say "Amen." ("Amen.")
If you're happy and you know it, say "Amen." ("Amen.")
If you're happy and you know it, then your face will surely show it.
If you're happy and you know it, say "Amen." ("Amen.")

It's the Hard-Knock Life

from the Musical Production ANNIE
Lyric by Martin Charnin
Music by Charles Strouse

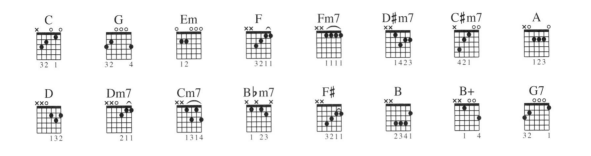

Strum Pattern: 4
Pick Pattern: 3

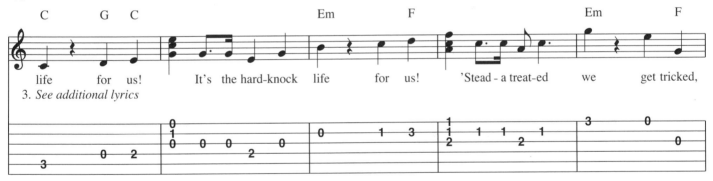

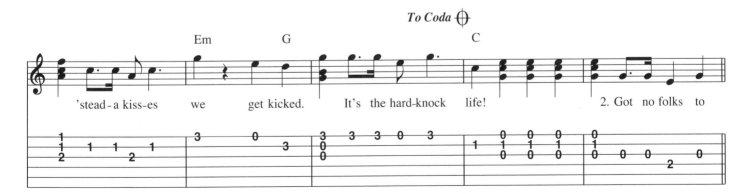

Verse

speak of, so, _____ it's the hard-knock row we hoe. _____ Cot-ton blan-kets 'stead-a wool,

_____ emp-ty bel-lies 'stead-a full, _____ it's the hard-knock life. Don't it

Bridge

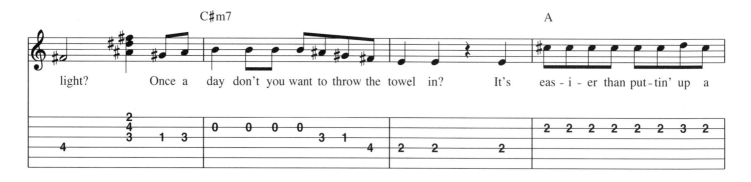

feel like the wind is al-ways howl-in'? Don't it seem like there's nev-er an-y

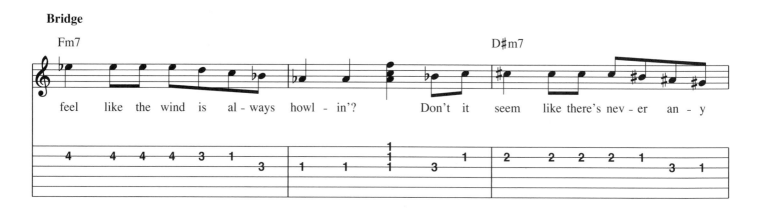

light? Once a day don't you want to throw the towel in? It's eas-i-er than put-tin' up a

fight. No one's there when your dreams at night get creep-y. No one

cares if you grow, or if you shrink. No one dries when your eyes get wet and

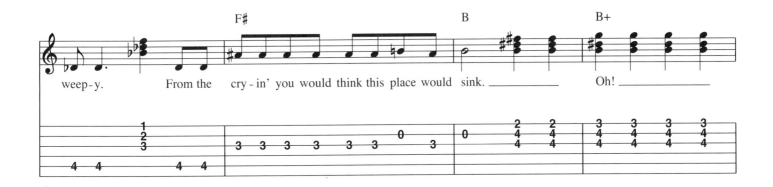

weep-y. From the cry-in' you would think this place would sink. _____ Oh! _____

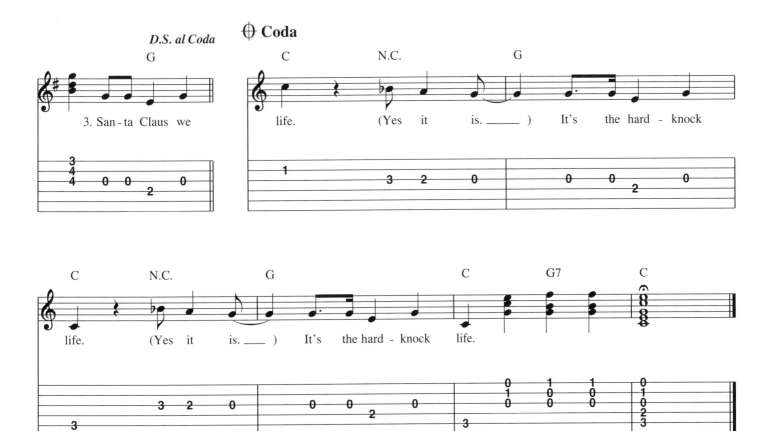

D.S. al Coda

⊕ Coda

3. San-ta Claus we

life. (Yes it is. ___) It's the hard - knock

life. (Yes it is. ___) It's the hard - knock life.

Additional Lyrics

3. Santa Claus we never see,
Santa Claus, what's that? Who's he?
No one cares for you a smidge
When you're in an orphanidge.
It's the hard-knock life. (Yes it is.)
It's the hard-knock life. (Yes it is.)
It's the hard-knock life.

The Inch Worm

from the Motion Picture HANS CHRISTIAN ANDERSEN

By Frank Loesser

Chorus

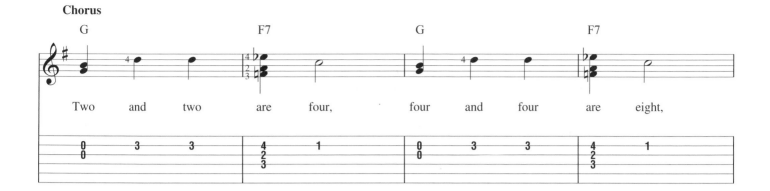

Two and two are four, four and four are eight,

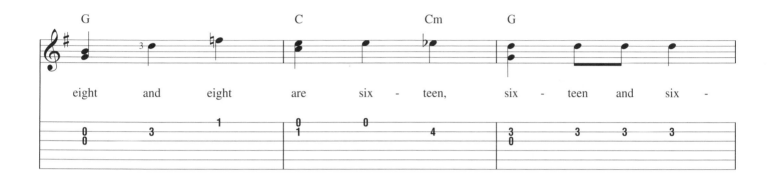

eight and eight are six - teen, six - teen and six -

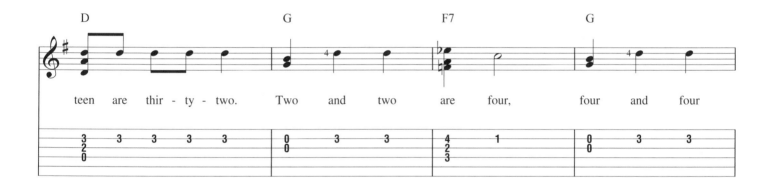

teen are thir - ty - two. Two and two are four, four and four

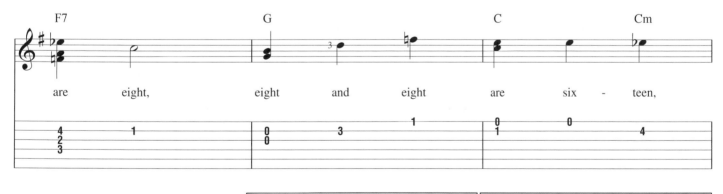

are eight, eight and eight are six - teen,

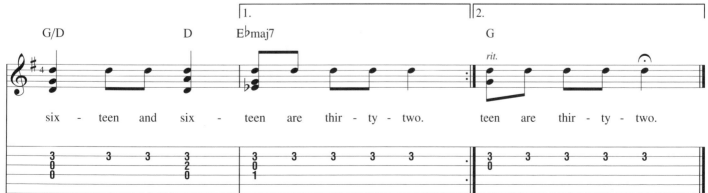

six - teen and six - teen are thir - ty - two. teen are thir - ty - two.

Linus and Lucy

from A BOY NAMED CHARLIE BROWN

By Vince Guaraldi

*Capo IV

Strum Pattern: 5
Pick Pattern: 5

*Optional: To match recording, place capo at the 4th fret.
**Chord symbols reflect implied harmony.

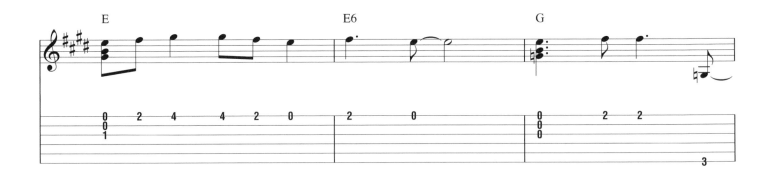

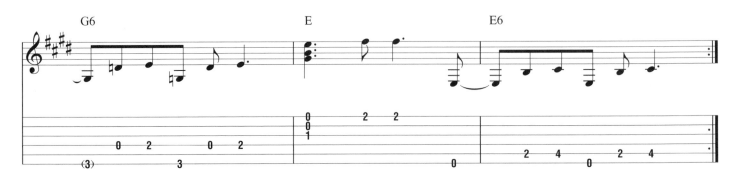

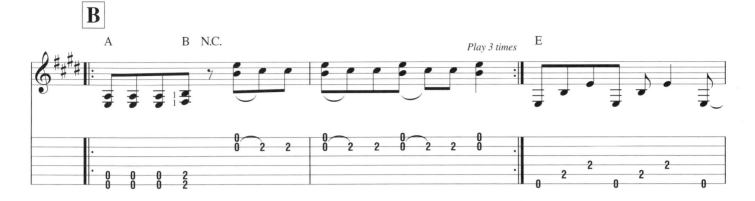

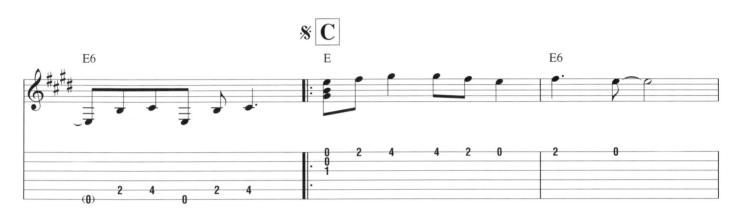

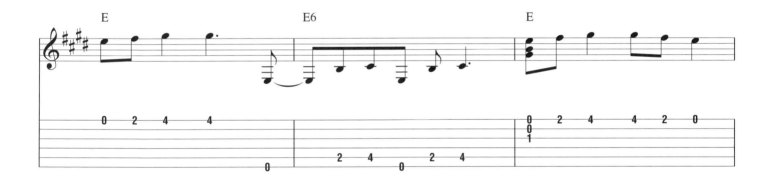

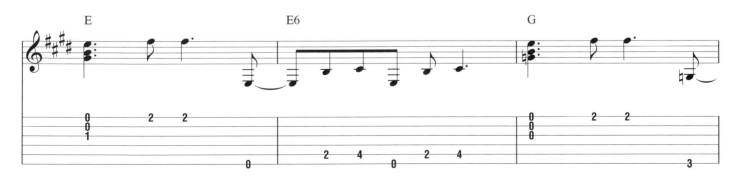

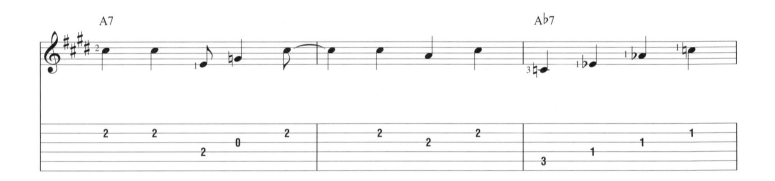

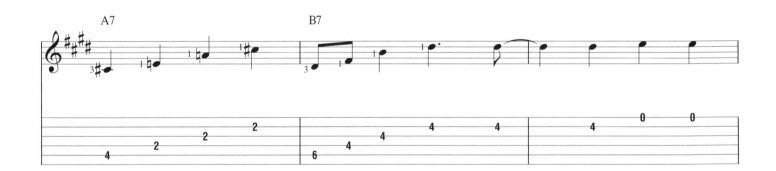

2nd time, D.S. al Coda

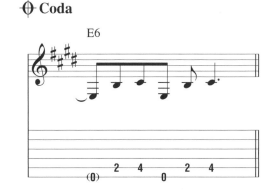Coda

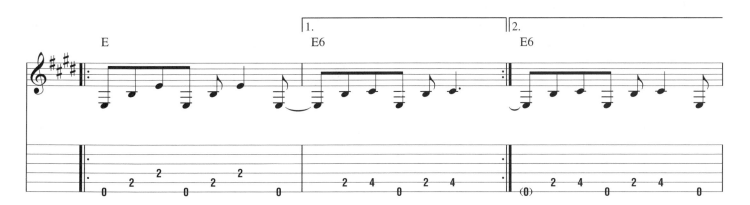

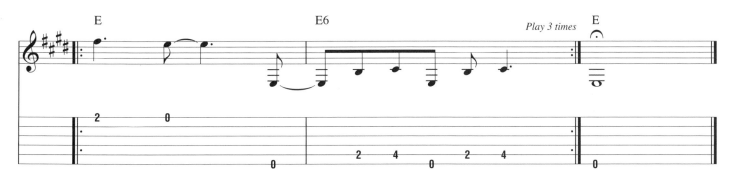

Little People

from LES MISERABLES

Music by Claude-Michel Schönberg
Lyrics by Alain Boublil, Jean-Marc Natel and Herbert Kretzmer

*Strum Pattern: 3
*Pick Pattern: 3

*Use Pattern 10 for 2/4 measures.

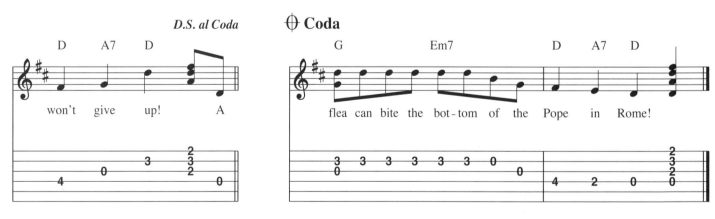

Additional Lyrics

2. Goliath was a bruiser who was tall as the sky,
   But David threw a right and gave him one in the eye.
   I never read the Bible but I know that it's true,
   Only goes to show what little people can do.

Mah-Nà Mah-Nà

By Piero Umiliani

Strum Pattern: 1
Pick Pattern: 1

The Lonely Goatherd

from THE SOUND OF MUSIC
Lyrics by Oscar Hammerstein II
Music by Richard Rodgers

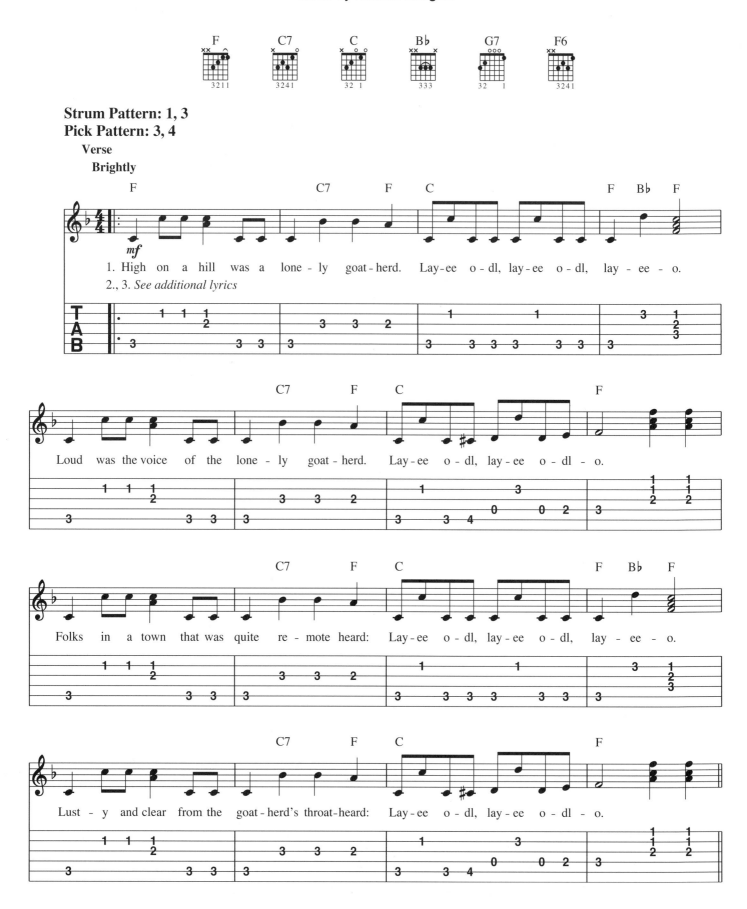

Strum Pattern: 1, 3
Pick Pattern: 3, 4

Verse
Brightly

1. High on a hill was a lone - ly goat - herd. Lay - ee o - dl, lay - ee o - dl, lay - ee - o.
2., 3. *See additional lyrics*

Loud was the voice of the lone - ly goat - herd. Lay - ee o - dl, lay - ee o - dl - o.

Folks in a town that was quite re - mote heard: Lay - ee o - dl, lay - ee o - dl, lay - ee - o.

Lust - y and clear from the goat - herd's throat - heard: Lay - ee o - dl, lay - ee o - dl - o.

Chorus

Additional Lyrics

2. A prince on the bridge of a castle moat heard:
   Lay-ee o-di, lay-ee o-di, lay-ee-o.
   Men on a road with a load to tote, heard:
   Lay-ee o-di, lay-ee o-di-o.
   Men in the midst of a table d'hote heard:
   Lay-ee o-di, lay-ee o-di, lay-ee-o.
   Men drinkin' beer with the foam a float, heard:
   Lay-ee o-di, lay-ee o-di-o.

3. One little girl in a pale pink coat heard:
   Lay-ee o-di, lay-ee o-di, lay-ee-o.
   She yodled back to the lonely goatherd,
   Lay-ee o-di, lay-ee o-di-o.
   Soon her name with a gleaming gloat heard:
   Lay-ee o-di, lay-ee o-di, lay-ee-o.
   What a duet for a girl and a goatherd.
   Lay-ee o-di, lay-ee o-di-o.

Love Me Tender

Words and Music by Elvis Presley and Vera Matson

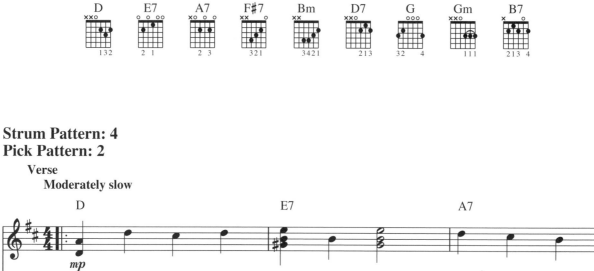

Strum Pattern: 4
Pick Pattern: 2

Verse
Moderately slow

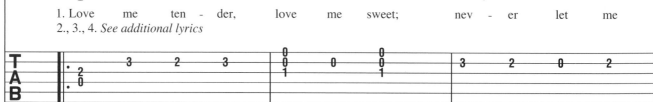

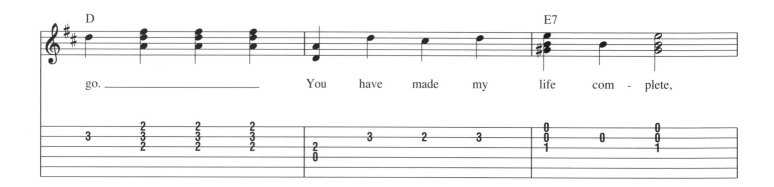

1. Love me ten - der, love me sweet; nev - er let me
2., 3., 4. *See additional lyrics*

go. _____ You have made my life com - plete,

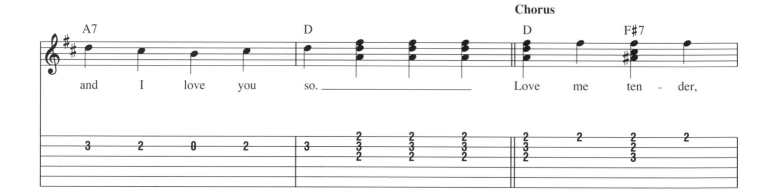

and I love you so. _____ Love me ten - der,

love me true. All my dreams ful - fill. _____

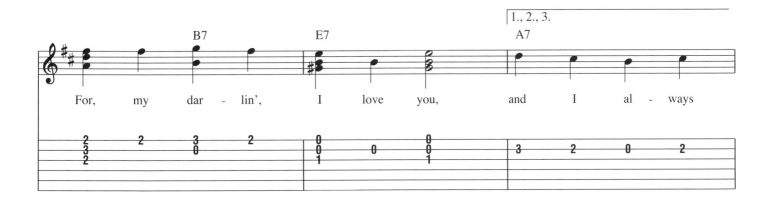

1., 2., 3.

For, my dar - lin', I love you, and I al - ways

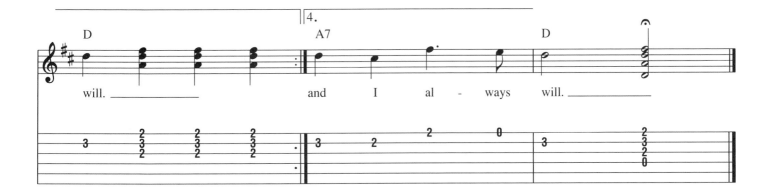

4.

will. _____ and I al - ways will. _____

Additional Lyrics

2. Love me tender, love me long;
   Take me to your heart.
   For it's there that I belong;
   And we'll never part.

3. Love me tender, love me dear;
   Tell me you are mine.
   I'll be yours through all the years,
   Till the end of time.

4. When at last my dreams come true,
   Darling, this I know:
   Happiness will follow you,
   Ev'rywhere you go.

Mairzy Doats

Words and Music by Milton Drake, Al Hoffman and Jerry Livingston

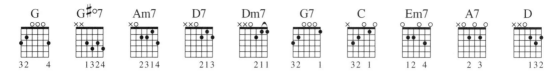

Strum Pattern: 3
Pick Pattern: 3

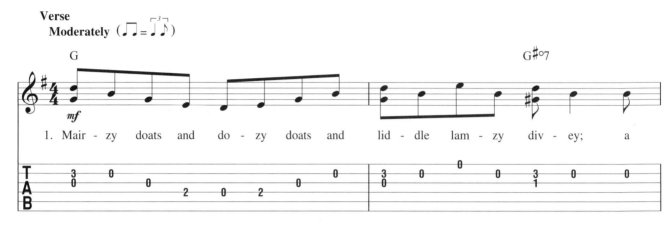

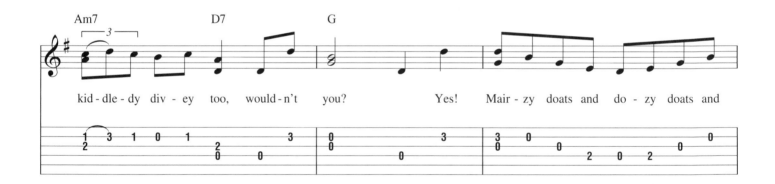

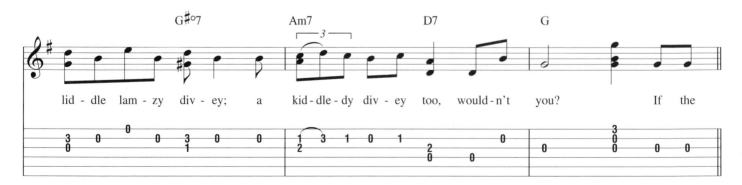

Bridge

words sound queer and fun - ny to your ear, a lit - tle bit jum - bled and

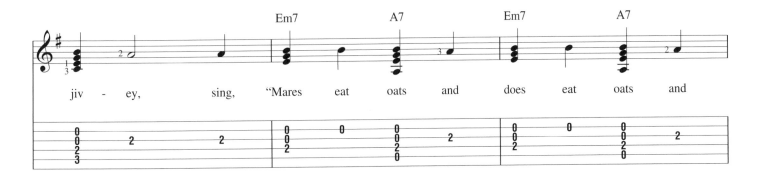

jiv - ey, sing, "Mares eat oats and does eat oats and

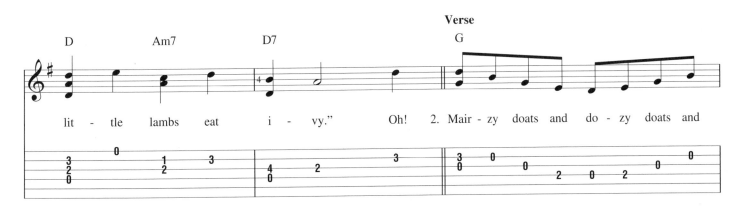

Verse

lit - tle lambs eat i - vy." Oh! 2. Mair - zy doats and do - zy doats and

lid - dle lam - zy div - ey; a kid - dle - dy div - ey too, would - n't

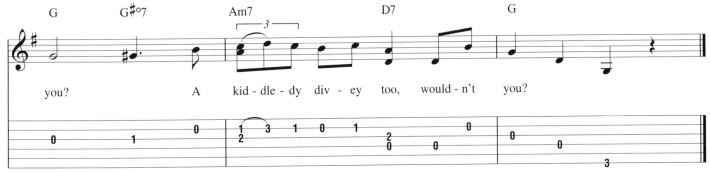

you? A kid - dle - dy div - ey too, would - n't you?

Maybe

from the Musical Produciton ANNIE
Lyric by Martin Charnin
Music by Charles Strouse

www.CharlesStrouse.com

Additional Lyrics

2. Maybe in a house
All hidden by a hill,
She's sitting playing pianah,
He's sitting paying a bill.

Bridge Betcha he reads, betcha she sews.
Maybe she's made me a closet of clothes.
Maybe they're strict, as straight as a line.
Don't really care as long as they're mine.

4. So, maybe now this prayer's
The last one of it's kind;
Won't you please come get your
Baby, maybe.

The Muppet Show Theme

from the Television Series
Words and Music by Jim Henson and Sam Pottle

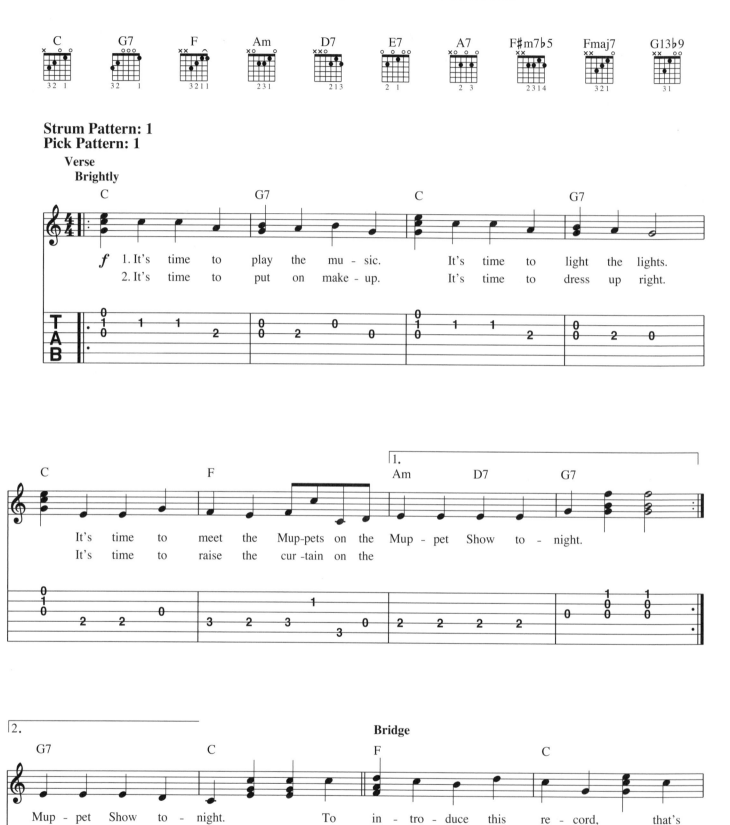

Strum Pattern: 1
Pick Pattern: 1

Verse
Brightly

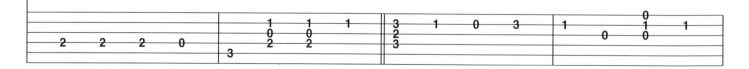

1. It's time to play the mu - sic. It's time to light the lights.
2. It's time to put on make - up. It's time to dress up right.

It's time to meet the Mup-pets on the Mup - pet Show to - night.
It's time to raise the cur -tain on the

Mup - pet Show to - night. To in - tro - duce this re - cord, that's

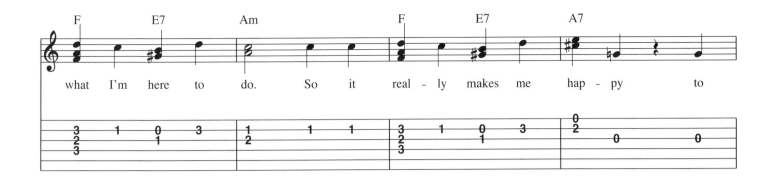

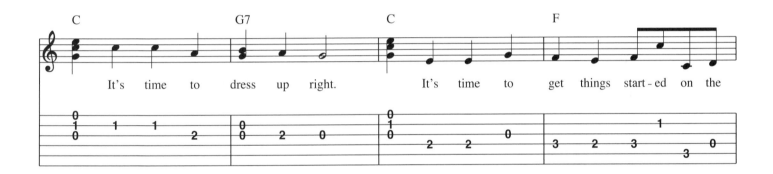

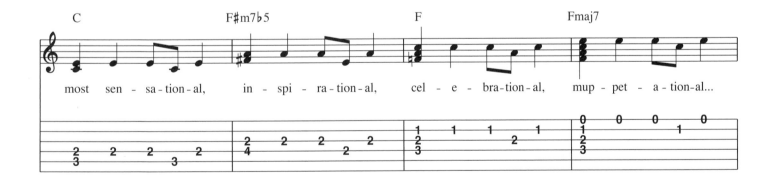

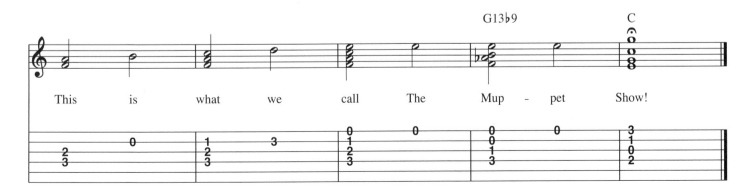

My Country, 'Tis of Thee

(America)

Words by Samuel Francis Smith
Music from Thesaurus Musicus

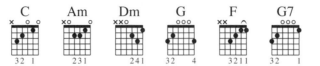

Strum Pattern: 7
Pick Pattern: 7

Verse
Moderately slow

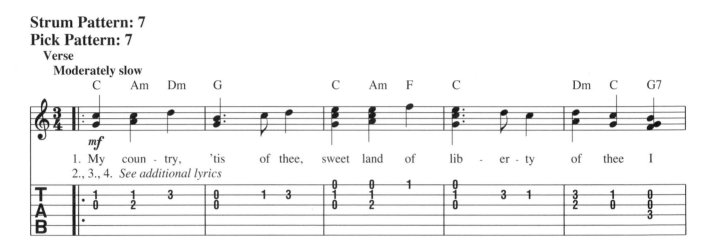

1. My coun - try, 'tis of thee, sweet land of lib - er - ty of thee I
2., 3., 4. *See additional lyrics*

sing. _____ Land where my fa - thers died! Land of the Pil - grims' pride!

From ev - 'ry _ moun - tain side, let _ free - dom ring! Great _ God, our King! _____

Additional Lyrics

2. My native country, thee,
   Land of the noble free,
   Thy name I love.
   I love thy rocks and rills,
   Thy woods and templed hills.
   My heart with rapture thrills
   Like that above.

3. Let music swell the breeze
   And ring from all the trees
   Sweet freedom's song.
   Let mortal tongues awake;
   Let all that breathe partake;
   Let rocks their silence break,
   The sound prolong.

4. Our fathers' God, to Thee
   Author of liberty,
   To Thee we sing.
   Long may our land be bright
   With freedom's holy light;
   Protect us by Thy might,
   Great God, our King!

On the Good Ship Lollipop

Words and Music by Sidney Clare and Richard A. Whiting

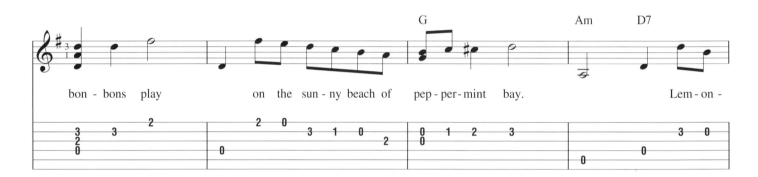

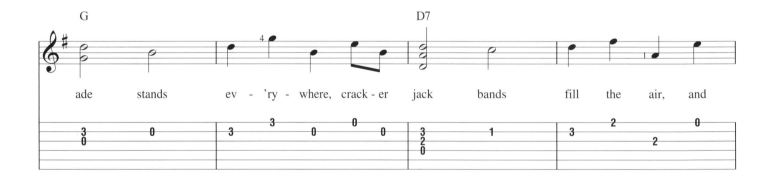

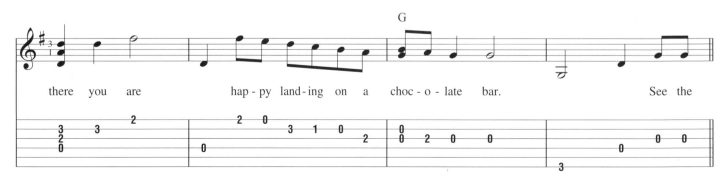

Bridge

sug - ar bowl do a toot - sie roll with the big bad dev - il's food

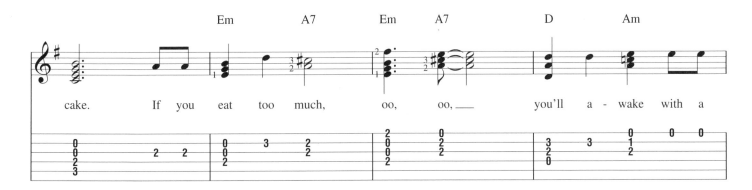

cake. If you eat too much, oo, oo, ___ you'll a - wake with a

Verse

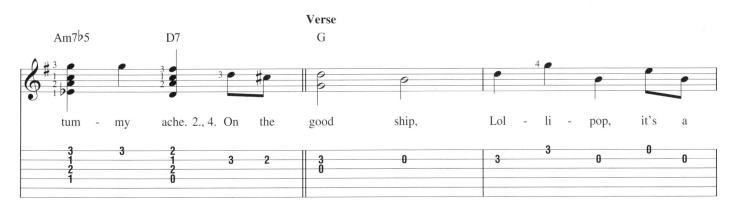

tum - my ache. 2., 4. On the good ship, Lol - li - pop, it's a

night trip in - to bed you hop and dream a - way on the good ship

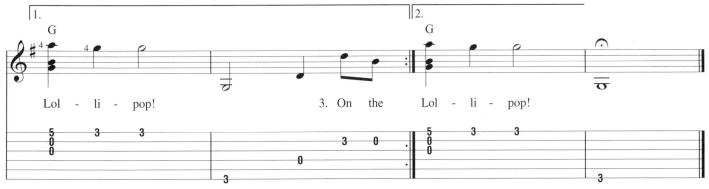

Lol - li - pop! 3. On the Lol - li - pop!

The Name Game

Words and Music by Lincoln Chase and Shirley Elliston

Strum Pattern: 2
Pick Pattern: 4

Intro
Fast

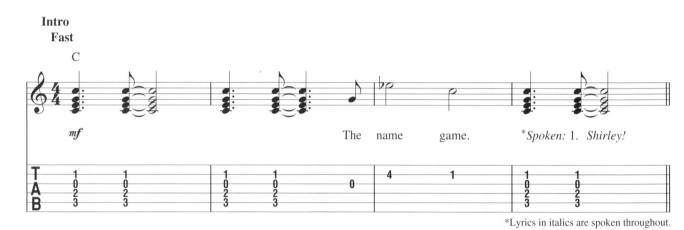

The name game. *Spoken: 1. Shirley!*

Lyrics in italics are spoken throughout.

Verse

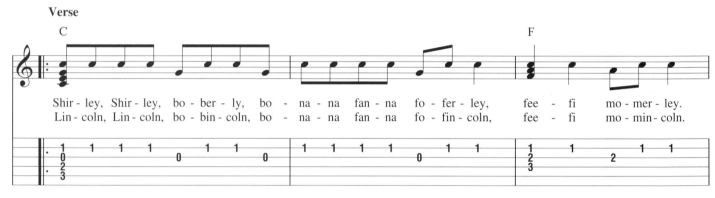

Shir - ley, Shir - ley, bo - ber - ly, bo - na - na fan - na fo - fer - ley, fee - fi mo - mer - ley.
Lin - coln, Lin - coln, bo - bin - coln, bo - na - na fan - na fo - fin - coln, fee - fi mo - min - coln.

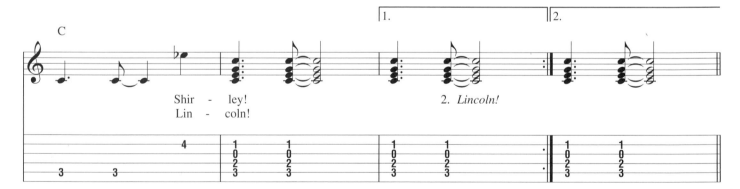

Shir - ley!
Lin - coln!

2. Lincoln!

Breakdown

Come on ev - 'ry - bod - y.
let - ter of the name,

I say now let's play a game.
I treat it like it was - n't there.

I bet - cha I can make a rhyme out of
But a B or an F or an

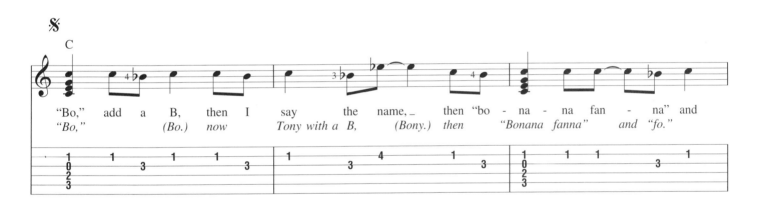

an - y - bod - y's name. The first And then I say,
M will ap - pear.

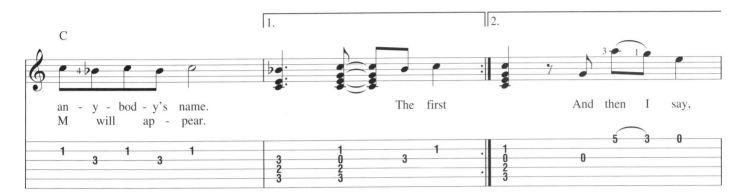

"Bo," add a B, then I say the name,_ then "bo - na - na fan - na" and
"Bo," (Bo.) now Tony with a B, (Bony.) then "Bonana fanna" and "fo."

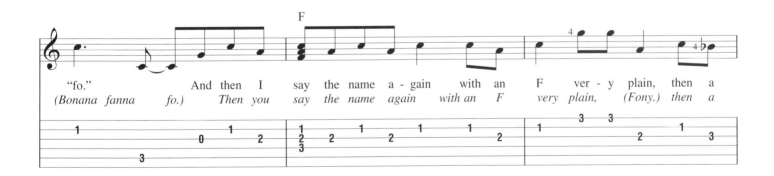

"fo." And then I say the name a - gain with an F ver - y plain, then a
(Bonana fanna fo.) Then you say the name again with an F very plain, (Fony.) then a

"fee - fi" and a "mo." And then I say the name a - gain with an
"fee - fi" and a "mo." (Fee - fi mo.) Then you say the name again with an M

125

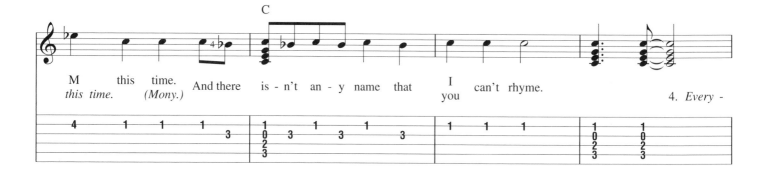

M   this time.   And there is - n't an - y name that   I can't rhyme.

this time.   *(Mony.)*   you   *4. Every -*

Verse

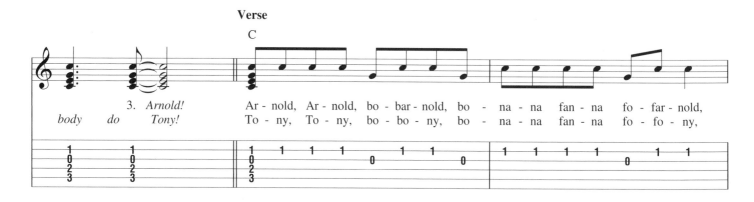

              3. Arnold!   Ar - nold, Ar - nold, bo - bar - nold, bo - na - na fan - na fo - far - nold,

body   *do*   *Tony!*   To - ny, To - ny, bo - bo - ny, bo - na - na fan - na fo - fo - ny,

To Coda ⊕

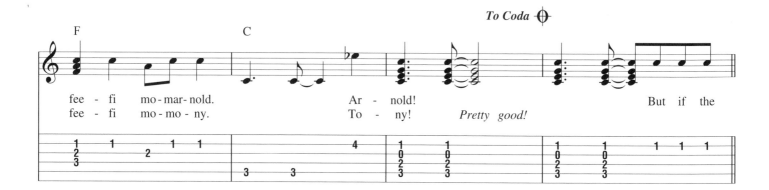

fee - fi mo - mar - nold.   Ar - nold!   But if the

fee - fi mo - mo - ny.   To - ny!   *Pretty good!*

Breakdown

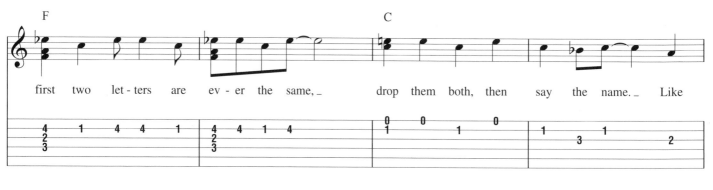

first two let - ters are ev - er the same, _   drop them both, then say the name. _ Like

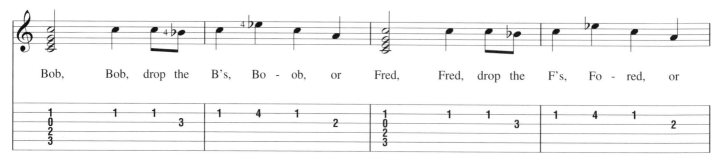

Bob,   Bob, drop the B's, Bo - ob, or   Fred,   Fred, drop the F's, Fo - red, or

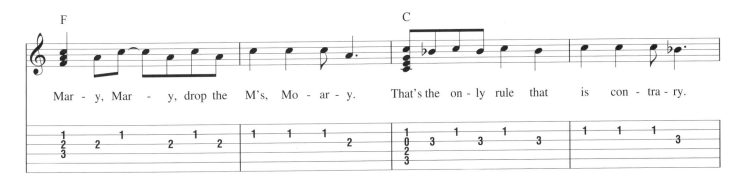

Mar - y, Mar - y, drop the M's, Mo - ar - y. That's the on - ly rule that is con - tra - ry.

D.S. al Coda

 Coda

Okay? Now say,

5. *Let's do Billy!*

Verse

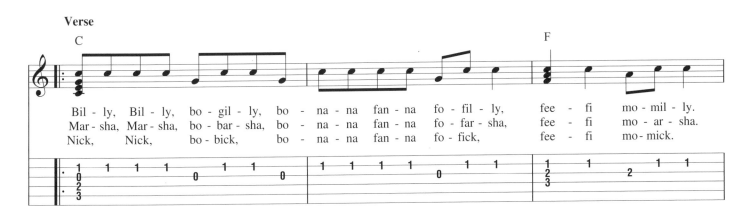

Bil - ly, Bil - ly, bo - gil - ly, bo - na - na fan - na fo - fil - ly, fee - fi mo - mil - ly.
Mar - sha, Mar - sha, bo - bar - sha, bo - na - na fan - na fo - far - sha, fee - fi mo - ar - sha.
Nick, Nick, bo - bick, bo - na - na fan - na fo - fick, fee - fi mo - mick.

1., 2. | 3.

Bil - ly! Very good. 6. *Let's do Marsha!* Nick!
Mar - sha! 7. A little trick with Nick!

Outro

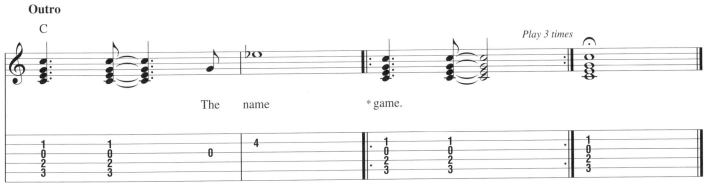

Play 3 times

The name *game.

*Sung 1st time only.

127

Over the Rainbow

from THE WIZARD OF OZ

Music by Harold Arlen
Lyric by E.Y. "Yip" Harburg

Strum Pattern: 3
Pick Pattern: 3

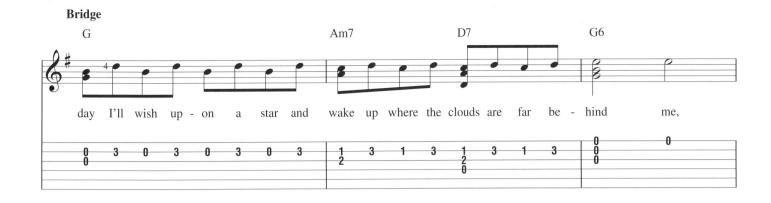

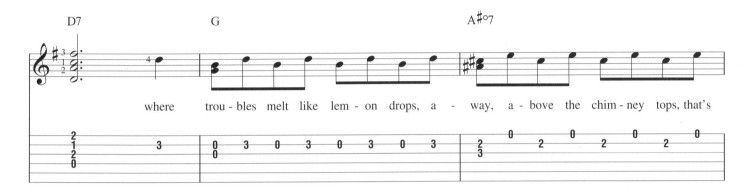

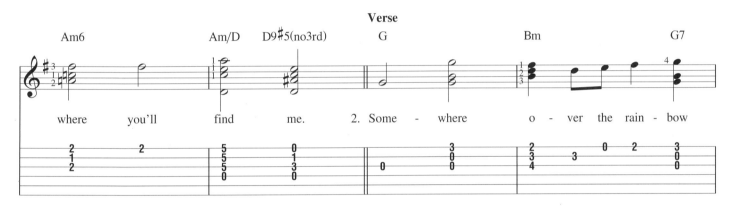

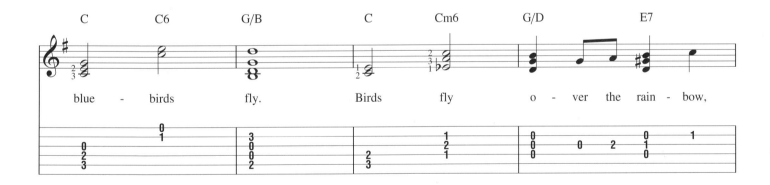

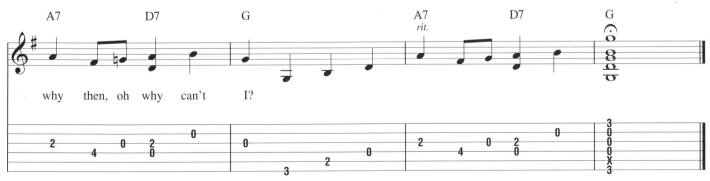

Over the River
and Through the Woods

Traditional

Strum Pattern: 8
Pick Pattern: 8

Verse
Briskly

1. O-ver the riv-er and through the woods, to grand-fa-ther's house we go; ___ the horse knows the way to
2., 3. *See additional lyrics*

car-ry the sleigh, through the white and drift-ed snow. _ O-ver the riv-er and through the words, oh how the wind does

blow! ___ It stings the toes and bites the nose as o-ver the ground we go. ___ pie!

Additional Lyrics

2. Over the river and through the woods,
To have a first-rate play;
Oh hear the bells ring, "Ting-a-ling-ling!"
Hurrah for Thanksgiving Day!
Over the river and through the woods,
Trot fast my dapple gray!
Spring over the gound like a hunting hound!
For this is Thanksgiving Day.

3. Over the river and through the woods,
And straight through the barnyard gate,
We seem to go extremely slow;
It is so hard to wait!
Over the river and through the woods,
Now grandmother's cap I spy!
Hurrah for the fun! Is the pudding done?
Hurrah for the pumpkin pie!

Part of Your World

from Walt Disney's THE LITTLE MERMAID

Music by Alan Menken
Lyrics by Howard Ashman

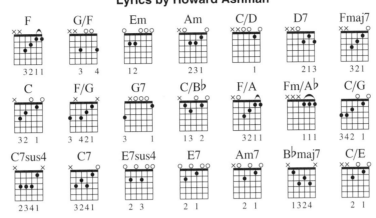

Strum Pattern: 5
Pick Pattern: 5

Verse
Moderately

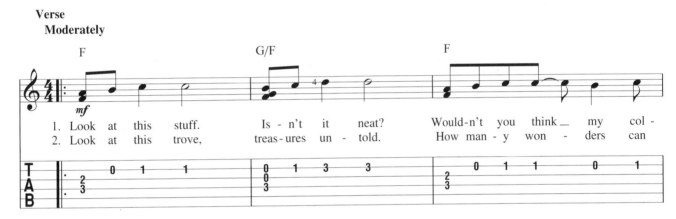

1. Look at this stuff. Is-n't it neat? Would-n't you think __ my col-
2. Look at this trove, treas-ures un - told. How man - y won - ders can

lec - tion's com - plete? Would-n't you think __ I'm the girl, the girl who has
one cav - ern hold? Look - ing a - round __ here you'd think, sure,

ev - 'ry - thing? she's got ev-'ry - thing. __ I've got

Pre-Chorus

gad - gets and giz - mos a - plen - ty. I've got who - zits and what - zits ga -

lore. You want thing - a - ma - bobs, I've got twen - ty. But who

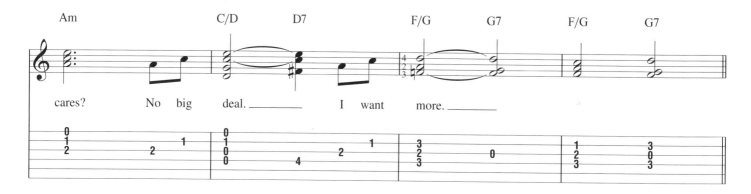

cares? No big deal. I want more.

Chorus

I wan - na be where the peo - ple are. I wan - na see, wan - na

see 'em danc - in', walk - in' a - round on those, what do you call 'em,

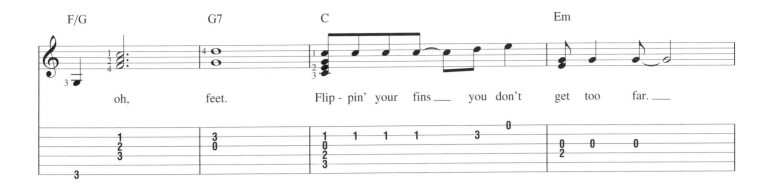

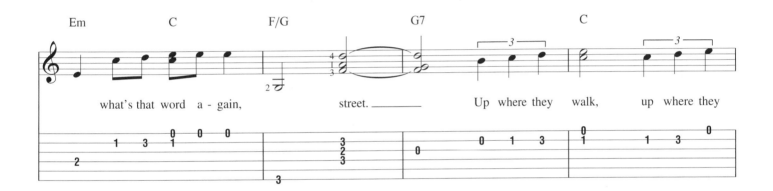

Bridge

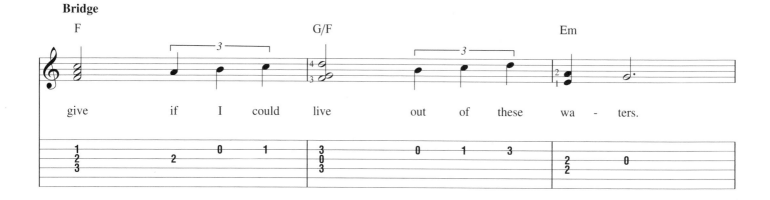

give   if   I   could   live   out   of   these   wa -   ters.

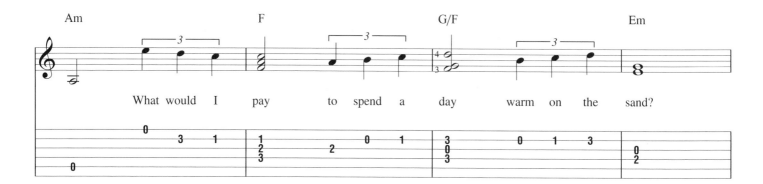

What would I   pay   to   spend a   day   warm on   the   sand?

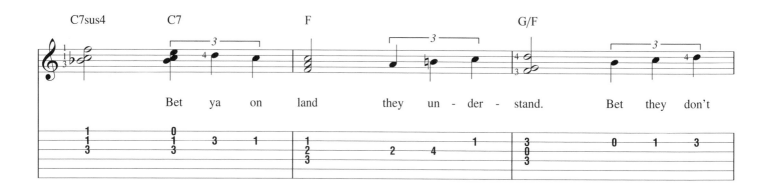

Bet   ya   on   land   they un - der - stand.   Bet they   don't

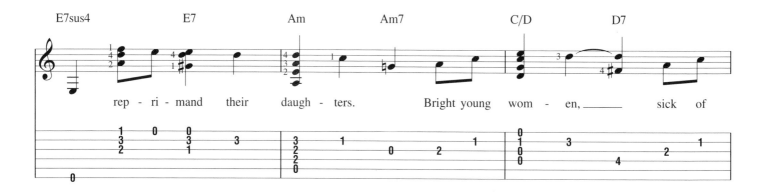

rep - ri - mand their daugh - ters.   Bright young wom - en,_____ sick of

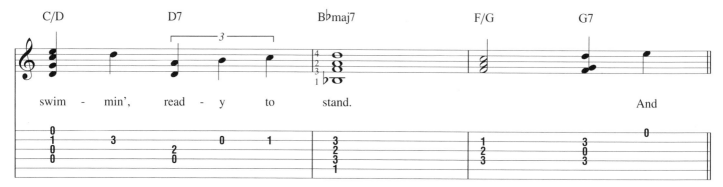

swim - min',   read - y   to   stand.   And

Outro-Chorus

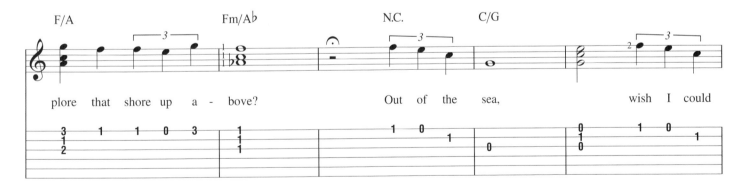

A Tempo

Peanut Sat on a Railroad Track

Traditional

Strum Pattern: 3, 2
Pick Pattern: 3, 4
Moderately

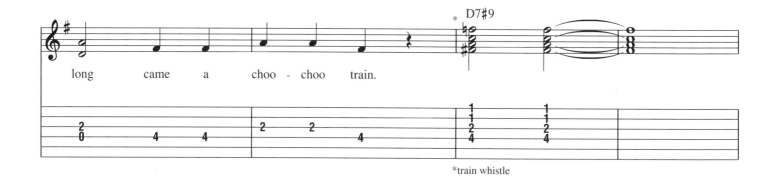

A pea - nut sat on a rail - road track, his heart was all a - flut - ter. A -

long came a choo - choo train.

*train whistle

Pea - nut _____ but - ter.

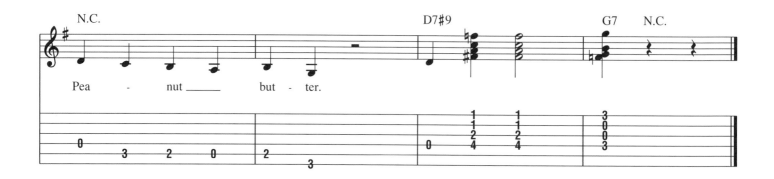

The Rainbow Connection

from THE MUPPET MOVIE

Words and Music by Paul Williams and Kenneth L. Ascher

Strum Pattern: 8, 9
Pick Pattern: 8, 9

Chorus

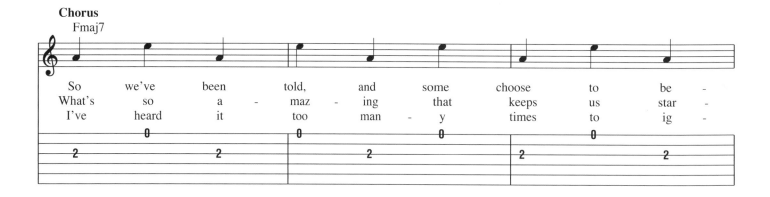

So we've been told, and some choose to be -
What's so a - maz - ing that keeps us star -
I've heard it too man - y times to ig -

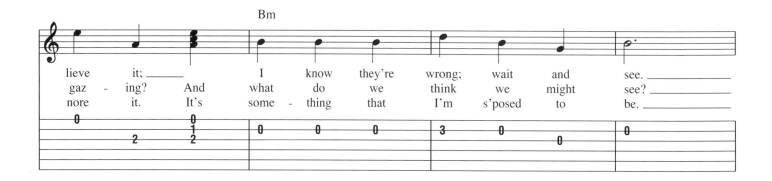

lieve it; _____ I know they're wrong; wait and see. _____
gaz - ing? And what do we think we might see? _____
nore it. It's some - thing that I'm s'posed to be. _____

Some - day we'll find it, _____ the rain - bow con -

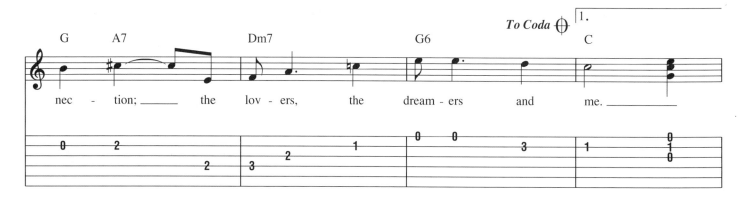

To Coda ⊕ | 1.

nec - tion; _____ the lov - ers, the dream - ers and me. _____

| 2.

me. _____

All of us un - der its spell; we know that it's

D.C. al Coda

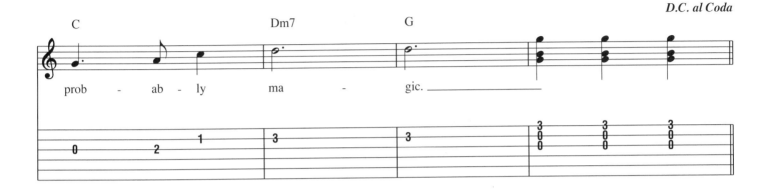

prob - ab - ly ma - gic. _____

⊕ **Coda**

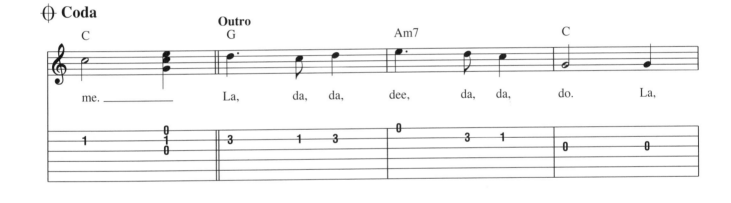

Outro

me. _____ La, da, da, dee, da, da, do. La,

la, da, da, da, de, da, do. _____

Additional Lyrics

2. Who said that ev'ry wish could be heard and answered
   When wished on the morning star?
   Somebody thought of that, and someone believed it;
   Look what it's done so far.

3. Have you been half asleep and then you heard voices?
   I've heard them calling my name.
   Is this the sweet sound that calls the young sailors?
   The voice might be one and the same.

People in Your Neighborhood

from the Television Series SESAME STREET

Words and Music by Jeff Moss

Strum Pattern: 3
Pick Pattern: 3

Intro
Moderately fast

Oh, _____

%**Chorus**

who are the peo - ple in your neigh - bor - hood, in your neigh - bor - hood, in your
post - man is a per - son in your neigh - bor - hood, in your neigh - bor - hood, in your
fire - man

To Coda ⊕

neigh - bor - hood? Say, who are the peo - ple in your neigh - bor - hood, the
neigh - bor - hood. A post - man is a per - son in your neigh - bor - hood, a
And a

peo - ple that you meet each day?
per - son that you meet each day.

Verse

1. Oh, the post - man al - ways brings the mail _____ through
2. Oh, a fire - man is brave, it's said. _____ His

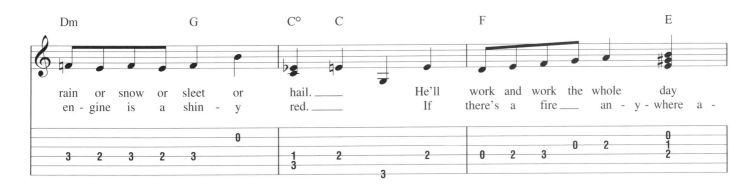

rain or snow or sleet or hail. _____ He'll work and work the whole day
en - gine is a shin - y red. _____ If there's a fire _____ an - y - where a -

D.S. al Coda

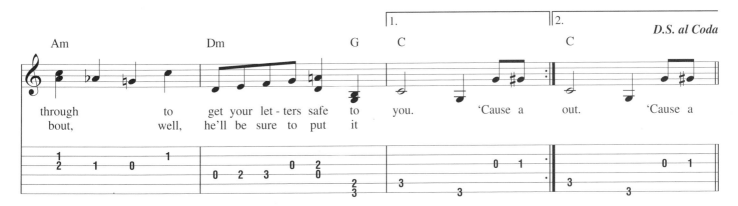

through to get your let - ters safe to you. 'Cause a out. 'Cause a
bout, well, he'll be sure to put it

Coda

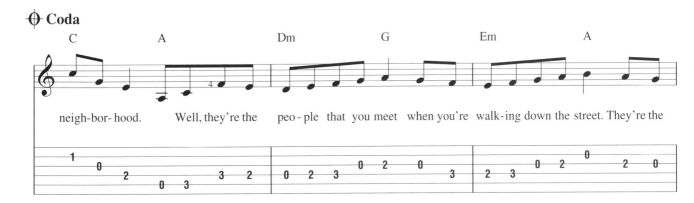

neigh-bor-hood. Well, they're the peo - ple that you meet when you're walk-ing down the street. They're the

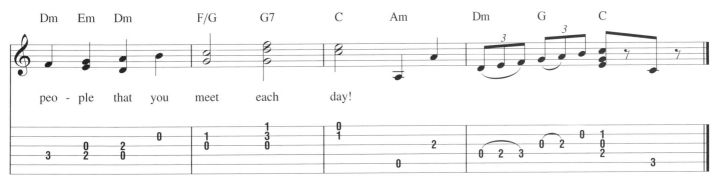

peo - ple that you meet each day!

141

Pure Imagination

from WILLY WONKA AND THE CHOCOLATE FACTORY

Words and Music by Leslie Bricusse and Anthony Newley

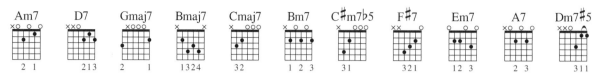

Strum Pattern: 3
Pick Pattern: 3

Verse

Slowly, in 2

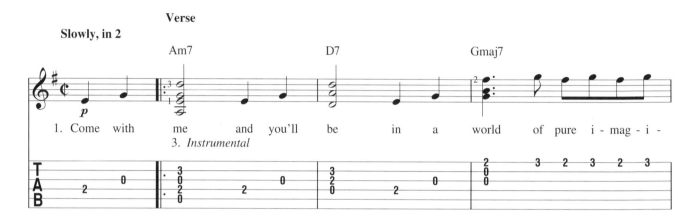

1. Come with me and you'll be in a world of pure i-mag-i-
3. *Instrumental*

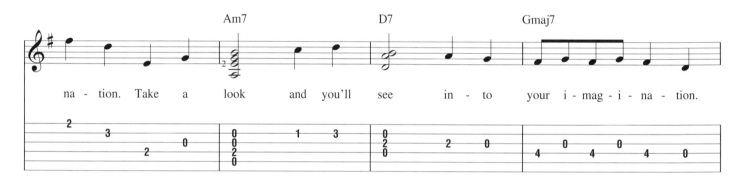

na-tion. Take a look and you'll see in-to your i-mag-i-na-tion.

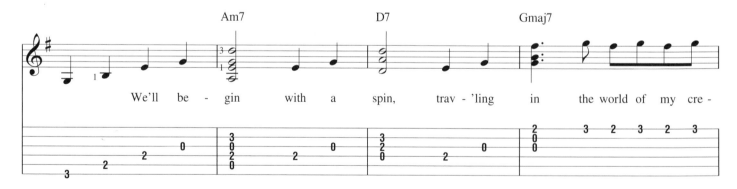

We'll be-gin with a spin, trav-'ling in the world of my cre-

a-tion. What we'll see will de-fy ex-pla-na-tion!

Bridge

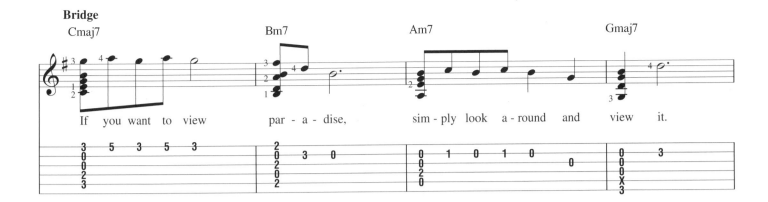

If you want to view par - a - dise, sim - ply look a - round and view it.

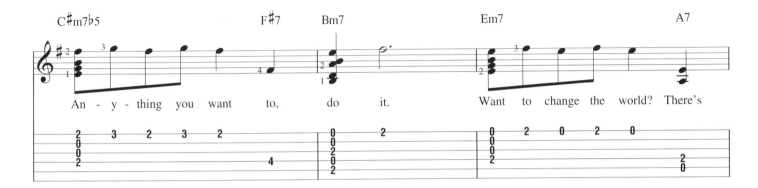

An - y - thing you want to, do it. Want to change the world? There's

Verse

noth - ing to it. 2., 4. There is no life I know to com -

pare with pure i - mag - i - na - tion. Liv - ing there, you'll be free if you

tru - ly wish to be. tru - ly wish to be.

Purple People Eater

Words and Music by Sheb Wooley

Strum Pattern: 2
Pick Pattern: 1

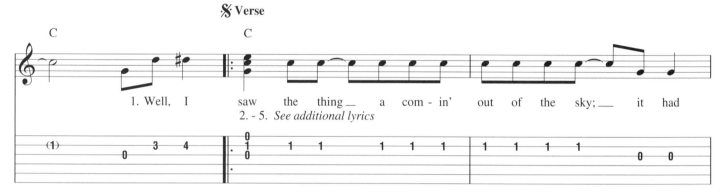

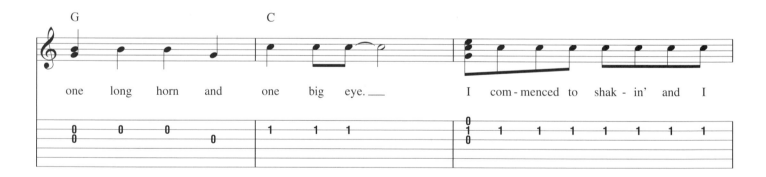

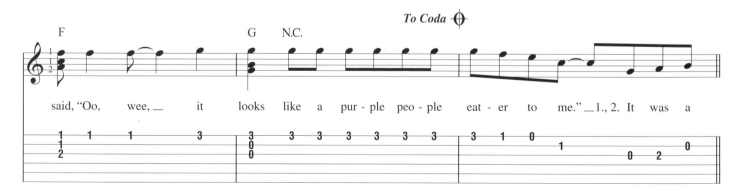

Chorus

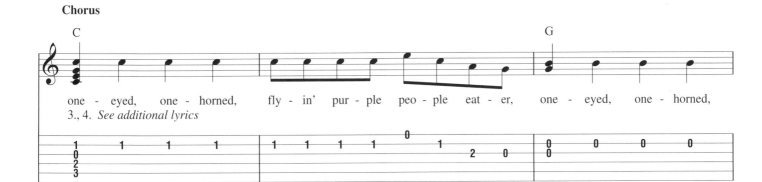

one - eyed, one - horned, fly - in' pur - ple peo - ple eat - er, one - eyed, one - horned,

3., 4. *See additional lyrics*

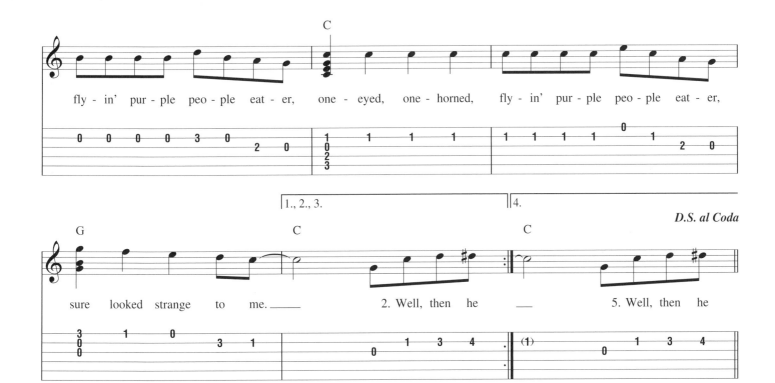

fly - in' pur - ple peo - ple eat - er, one - eyed, one - horned, fly - in' pur - ple peo - ple eat - er,

1., 2., 3.   4.

D.S. al Coda

sure looked strange to me. _____   2. Well, then he _____   5. Well, then he

Coda

horn in his head. _   *Spoken: Tequila!*

Additional Lyrics

2. Well, then he came down to earth and he lit in a tree.
   I said, "Mister purple people eater, don't eat me."
   I heard him say in a voice so gruff,
Spoken: "I wouldn't eat you 'cause you're so tough."

3. I said, "Mister purple people eater, what's your line?"
   He said, "Eatin' purple people, and it sure is fine,
   But that's not the reason that I came to land,
Spoken: I wanna get a job in a rock and roll band."

Chorus 3 Well, bless my soul, rock 'n' roll, flyin' purple people eater,
   Pigeon-toed, under-growed, flyin' purple people eater,
   He wears short shorts, friendly little people eater.
   What a sight to see.

4. And then he swung from the tree and he lit on the ground,
   And he started to rock, a really rockin' around.
   A crazy ditty with a swingin' tune,
   Singin' *Spoken: bop, bap a loop a lap a loom, bam, boom.*

Chorus 4 Well, bless my soul, rock 'n' roll, flyin' purple people eater,
   Pigeon-toed, under-growed, flyin' purple people eater,
Spoken: "I like short shorts!" friendly little people eater.
   What a sight to see.

5. Well, then he went on his way and then a what do you know,
   I saw him last night on the Star Out show.
   He was blowin' it out, really knockin' 'em dead,
   Playin' rock 'n' roll music thru the horn in his head.

The River Seine
(La Seine)

Words and Music by Allan Roberts and Alan Holt
Original French Text by Flavien Monod and Guy LaFarge

Strum Pattern: 8
Pick Pattern: 8

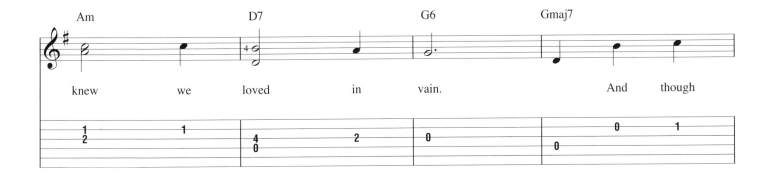

knew   we   loved   in   vain.   And   though

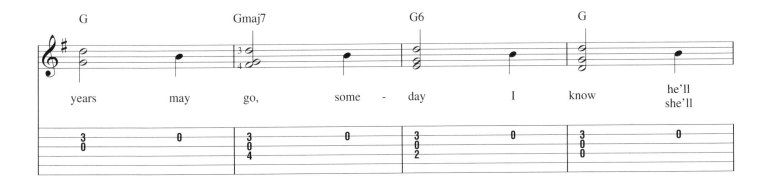

years   may   go,   some - day   I   know   he'll
she'll

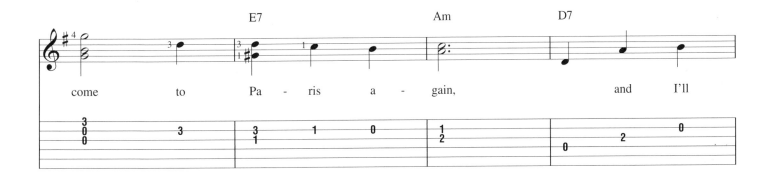

come   to   Pa - ris   a - gain,   and   I'll

find   him   where   I   lost   him   by   the   love - ly
her   her

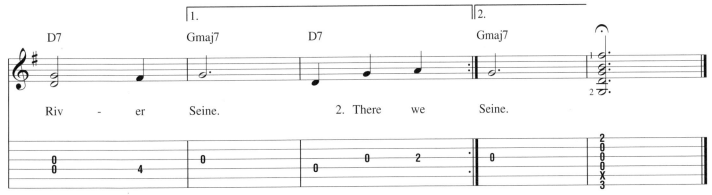

Riv - er   Seine.   2. There   we   Seine.

Rubber Duckie

from the Television Series SESAME STREET

Words and Music by Jeff Moss

Strum Pattern: 4
Pick Pattern: 4

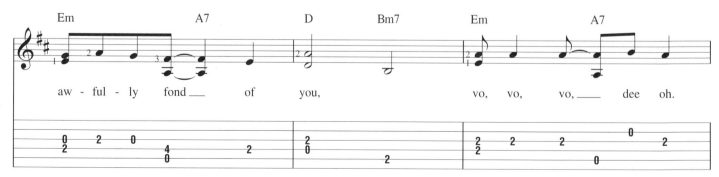

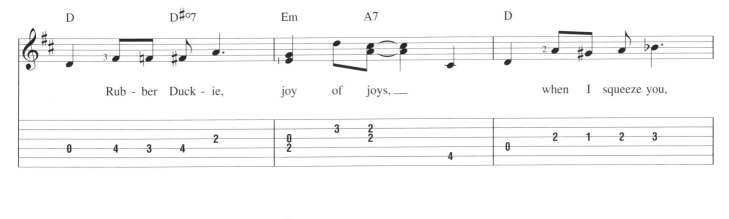

Rub - ber Duck - ie,   joy   of joys, ___   when   I squeeze you,

you   make   noise. ___   Rub - ber Duck - ie, you're my   ver - y best   friend,   it's

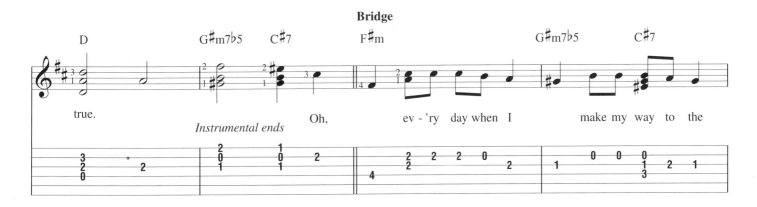

Bridge

true.   Oh,   ev - 'ry day when I   make my way   to the

Instrumental ends

tub - by, ___   I   find a   lit - tle fel - low who's

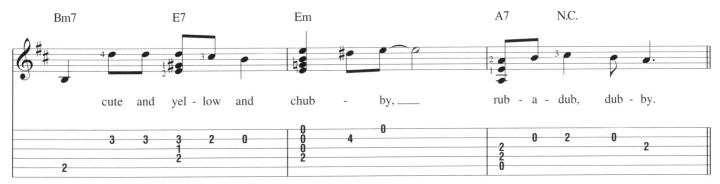

cute and yel - low and   chub - by, ___   rub - a - dub,   dub - by.

Verse

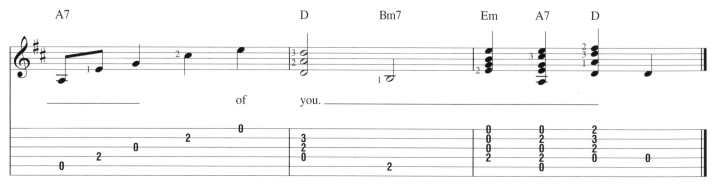

School Days
(When We Were a Couple of Kids)

Words by Will D. Cobb
Music by Gus Edwards

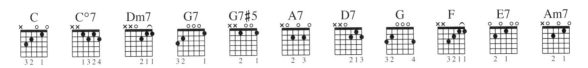

Strum Pattern: 7, 8
Pick Pattern: 8

Sesame Street Theme

Words by Bruce Hart, Jon Stone and Joe Raposo
Music by Joe Raposo

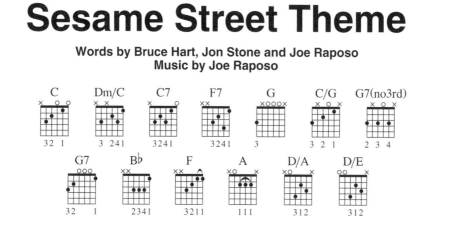

Strum Pattern: 3
Pick Pattern: 3

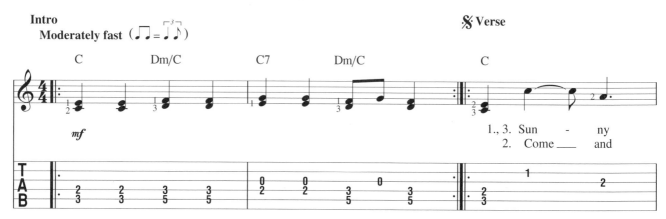

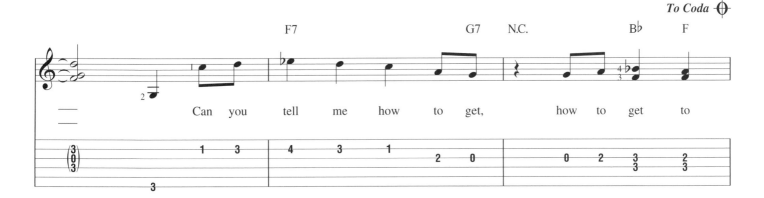

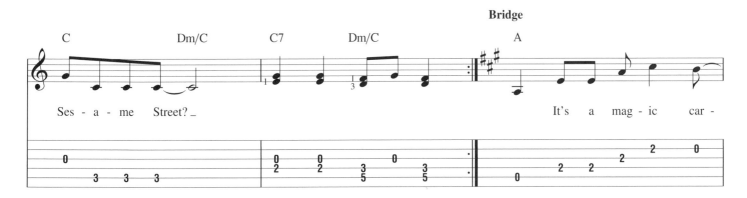

⊕ **Coda**

Repeat and fade

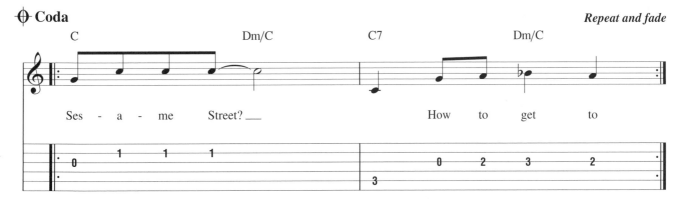

Sing

from SESAME STREET

Words and Music by Joe Raposo

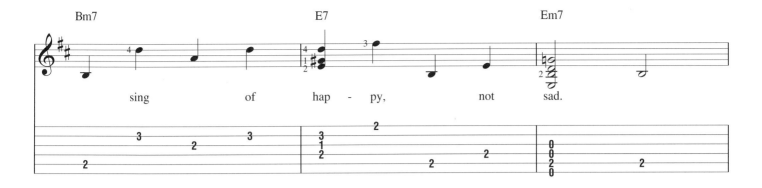

sing   of   hap - py,   not   sad.

Verse

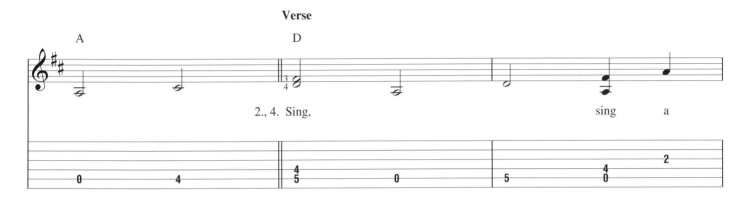

2., 4. Sing,   sing a

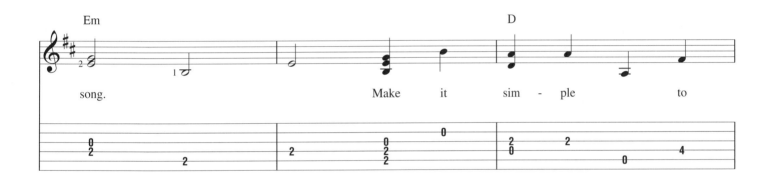

song.   Make   it   sim - ple   to

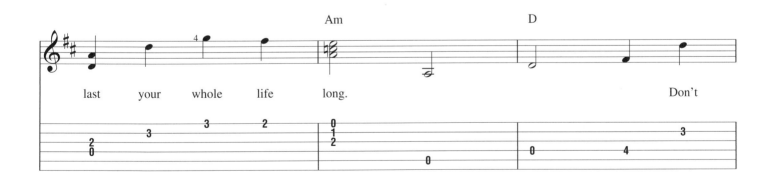

last   your   whole   life   long.   Don't

wor - ry   that   it's   not   good e - nough   for   an - y - one   else   to

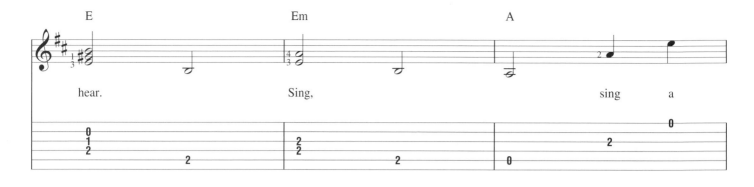

Interlude

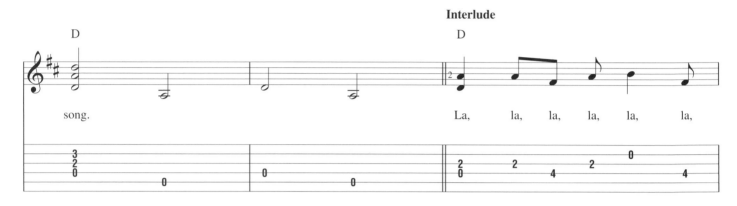

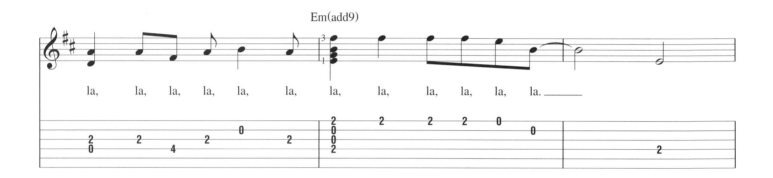

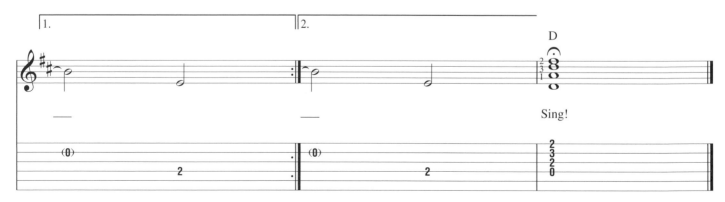

SpongeBob SquarePants Theme Song

from SPONGEBOB SQUAREPANTS

Words and Music by Mark Harrison, Blaise Smith, Steve Hillenburg and Derek Drymon

Strum Pattern: 1
Pick Pattern: 1

So Long, Farewell

from THE SOUND OF MUSIC

Lyrics by Oscar Hammerstein II
Music by Richard Rodgers

*Strum Pattern: 2, 3
*Pick Pattern: 2, 5

Moderately

Children:
There's a sad sort of clang-ing from the clock in the hall and the bells in the stee - ple

*Use Pattern 10 for 2/4 measures

too. _____ And up in the nurs-'ry an ab - surd lit - tle bird is pop-ping out to say, "Coo -

coo." _____ Re - gret-ful - ly they tell us, but firm-ly they com-pel us to
("Coo-coo." _)   ("Coo - coo." _____)   ("Coo - coo." .)   ("Coo - coo." _)

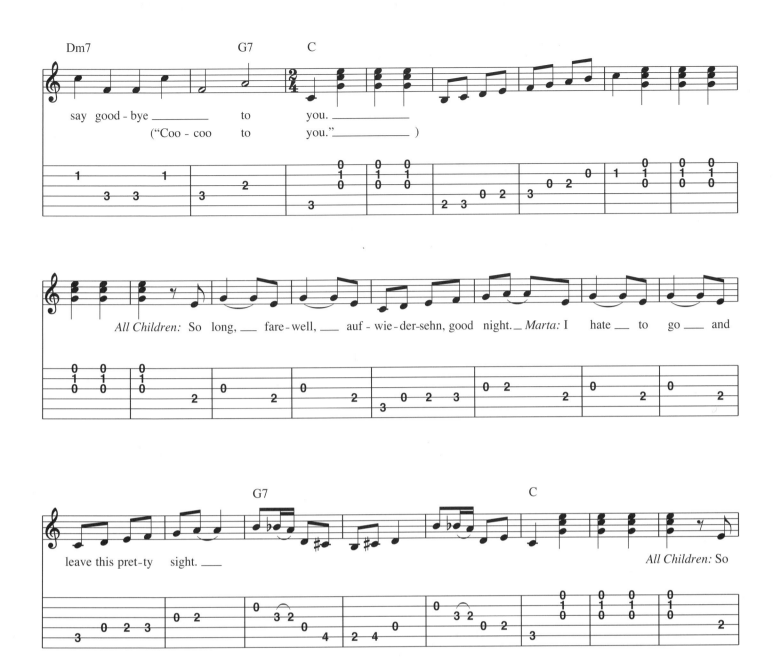

say good-bye _____ to you. _____ ("Coo-coo to you." _____)

All Children: So long, ___ fare-well, ___ auf-wie-der-sehn, good night. *Marta:* I hate ___ to go ___ and

leave this pret-ty sight. ___

All Children: So long, ___ fare-well, ___ auf-wie-der-sehn, a-dieu. *Kurt:* A-dieu, ___ a-dieu, ___ to

yieu and yieu and yieu. _____

All Children: So long, ___ fare - well, ___ au' - voir, auf - wie - der - sehn. _ Liesl: I'd

like ___ to stay ___ and taste my first cham - pagne. ___

All Children: So long, ___ fare - well, ___ auf - wie-der-sehn, good - bye. _ Friedrich: I

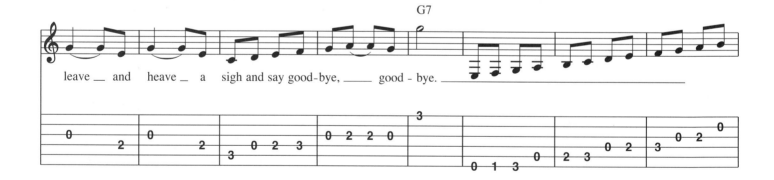

leave ___ and heave ___ a sigh and say good-bye, ___ good - bye. ___

Brigitta: I'm glad ___ to go, ___ I can-not tell a lie._ Louisa: I

flit, _____ I float, _____ I fleet - ly flee, I fly. _____

Slowly

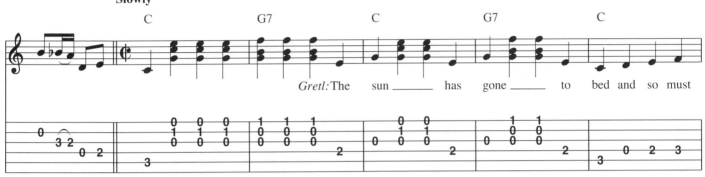

Gretl: The sun _____ has gone _____ to bed and so must

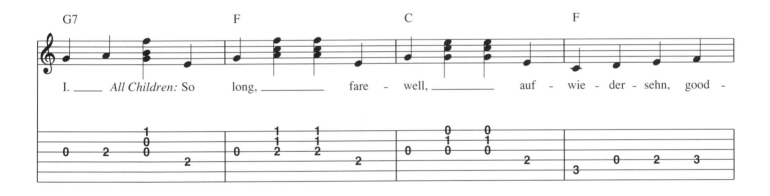

I. _____ *All Children:* So long, _____ fare - well, _____ auf - wie - der - sehn, good -

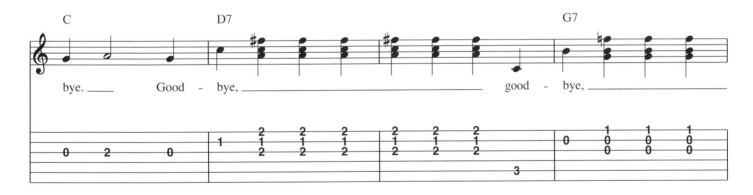

bye. _____ Good - bye, _____ good - bye, _____

_____ good - bye. _____ *Guests:* Good - bye!

Some Day My Prince Will Come

Words by Larry Morey
Music by Frank Churchill

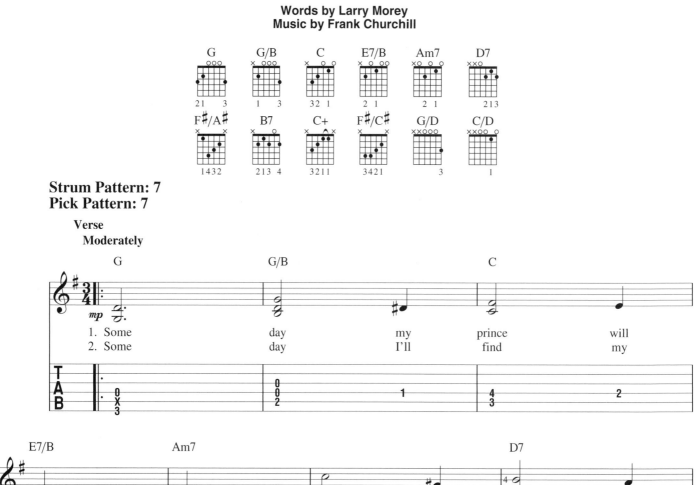

Strum Pattern: 7
Pick Pattern: 7

Verse
Moderately

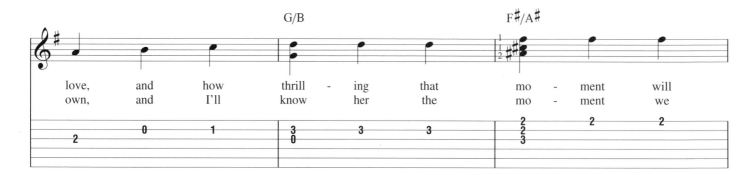

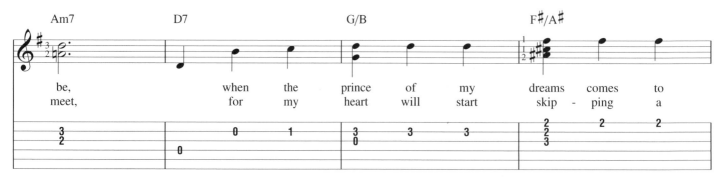

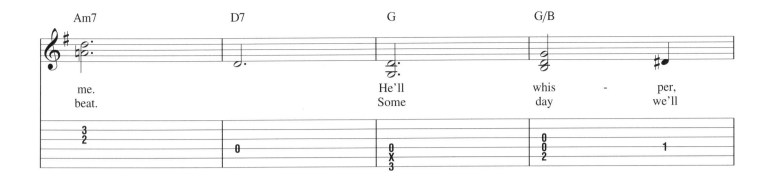

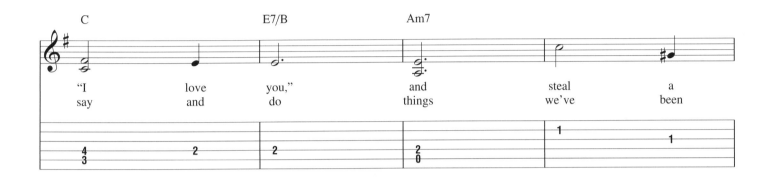

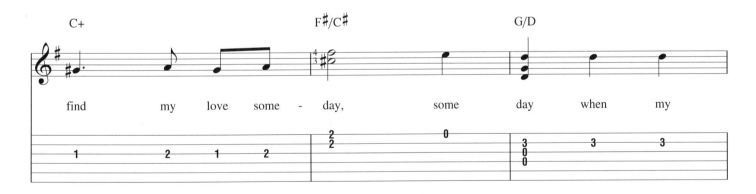

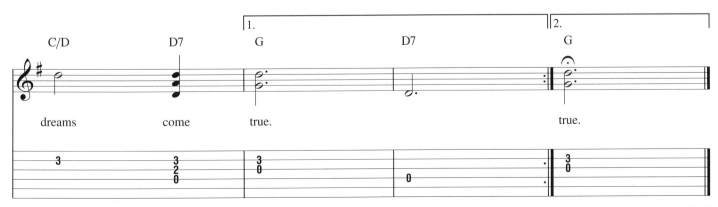

Splish Splash

Words and Music by Bobby Darin and Murray Kaufman

jumped back in the bath,_ well, how was I to know there was a par-ty go-ing on? on?_ I was a

Outro

splish-in' and a splash-in', I was a roll-in' and a stroll-in'. I was a

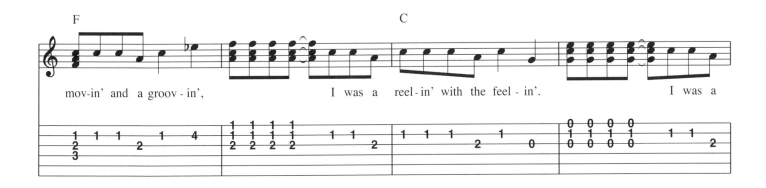

mov-in' and a groov-in', I was a reel-in' with the feel-in'. I was a

mov-in' and a groov-in', reel-in' with the feel-in'. Yeah, _____ splish, splash._

Additional Lyrics

2. Bing bang, I saw the whole gang,
Dancin' on my livin' room rug. Yeah.
Flip flop, they were doin' the bop,
All the teens had the dancin' bug.
There was Lollipop with Peggy Sue.
Good golly, Miss Molly was a even there too.
A well a splish splash, I forgot about the bath,
I went and put my dancing shoes on.

The Syncopated Clock

Music by Leroy Anderson
Words by Mitchell Parish

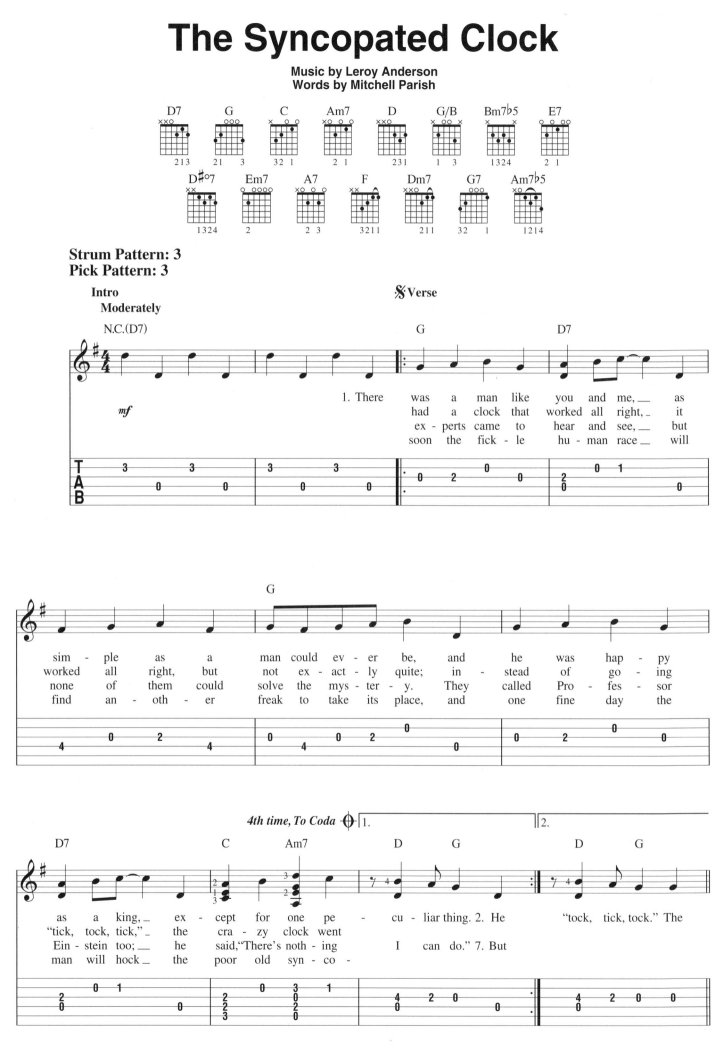

Bridge

poor old man just raved and raved,_ be - cause no - bod - y could say

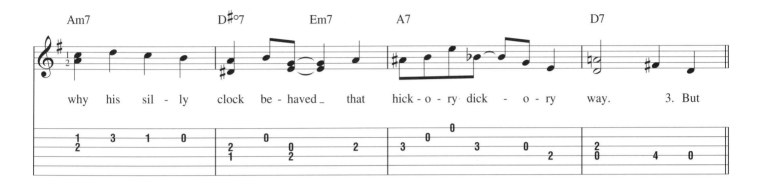

why his sil - ly clock be - haved _ that hick - o - ry dick - o - ry way. 3. But

Verse

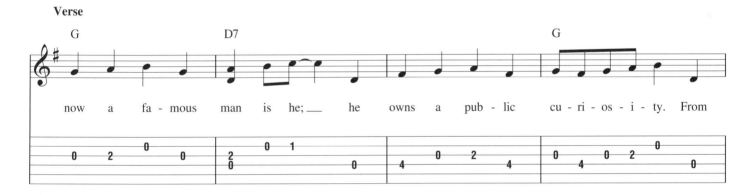

now a fa - mous man is he;_ he owns a pub - lic cu - ri - os - i - ty. From

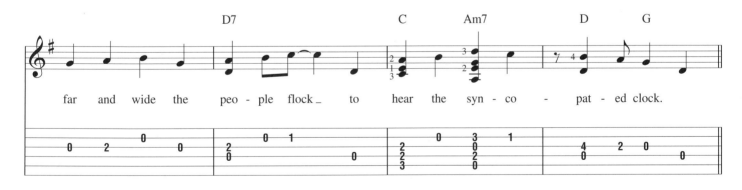

far and wide the peo - ple flock _ to hear the syn - co - pat - ed clock.

Interlude

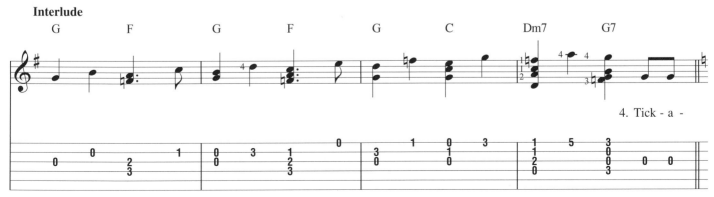

4. Tick - a -

Three Little Fishies

Words and Music by Saxie Dowell

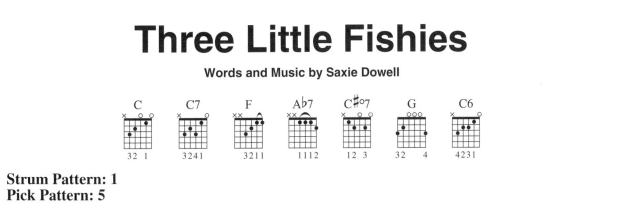

Strum Pattern: 1
Pick Pattern: 5

Intro
Moderately slow, in 2

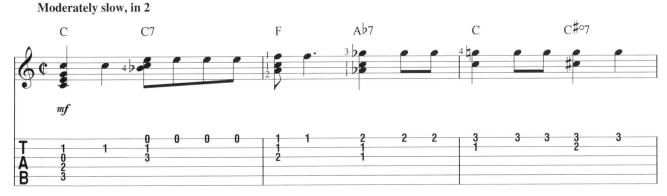

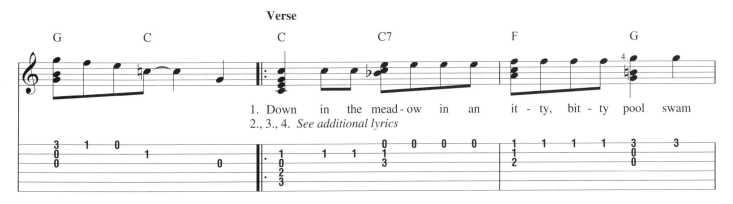

1. Down in the mead-ow in an it-ty, bit-ty pool swam
2., 3., 4. *See additional lyrics*

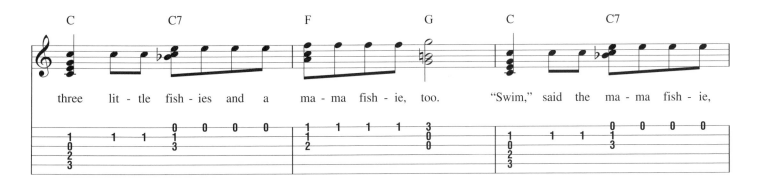

three lit-tle fish-ies and a ma-ma fish-ie, too. "Swim," said the ma-ma fish-ie,

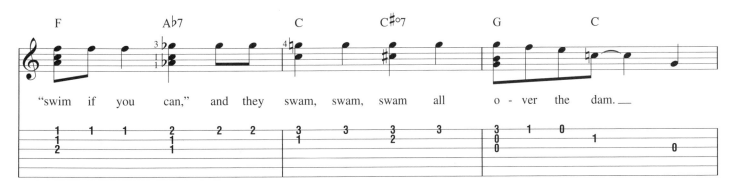

"swim if you can," and they swam, swam, swam all o-ver the dam. ___

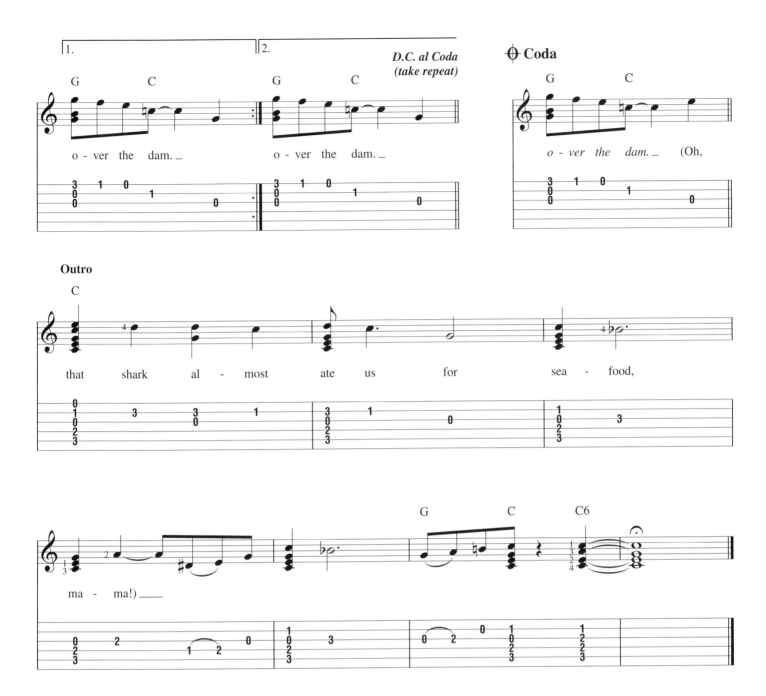

Additional Lyrics

2. "Stop," said the mama fishie, "or you'll get lost."
But the three little fishies didn't wanna be bossed.
So the three little fishies went out on a spree
And they swam, swam, swam right out to the sea.
("Top," taid the mama fiddie, "you'll get lost."
But the fwee wittow fishie didn't wanna be bossed.
The fwee wittow fishie went off on a spwee,
They fwam and they fwam wight off to the fea.)

Chorus 2 Boop, boo, riddle diddle dazzle, blip!
Boop, boo, riddle diddle dazzle, blip!
Boop, boo, riddle diddle dazzle, blip!
And they swam and they swam out to the sea.

3. "Wee!" yelled the fishies, "Oh, here's a lot of fun!
Swim in the sea till the day is done."
So they swam and they swam; it was all a lark
Till all of a sudden they met a shark.
("Wee!" yelled the wittow fishies, "Wots of fun!
We'll fwim in the fea till the day is done."
And they fwam and they fwam and it was a wark
Till all of a sudden they saw a shark.)

Chorus 3 Boop, boo, skiddly dit *(whistle)*, *bbpt!*
Boop, boo, skiddly dit *(whistle)*, bbpt!
Boop, boo, skiddly dit *(whistle)*, bbpt!
Till all of a sudden they saw a shark.

4. "Help!" cried the fishies, "Oh, look at the whales!"
Quick as they could, they turned on their tails.
Back to the pool in the meadow they swam
And swam and swam back over the dam.
("Help!" cried the wittow fishies, "Wook at the whales!"
Quick as they could, they turned on their tails.
Back to the poo in the meady they fwam
And they fwam and they fwam to the dam o dam.)

Chorus 4 Boop, boop, boo, boodiddle rackie sackie!
Boop, boop, boo, boodiddle rackie sackie!
Boop, boop, boo!
And they swam and they swam back over the dam.

*Sound effect with pursed lips.

This Land Is Your Land

Words and Music by Woody Guthrie

this land was made for you and me. This land is

Chorus

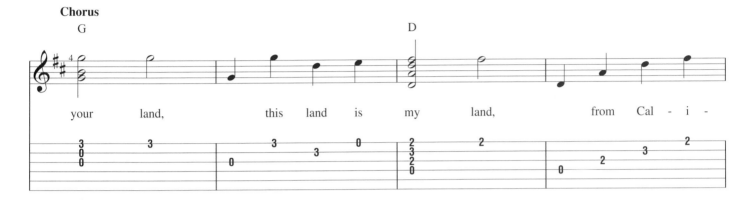

your land, this land is my land, from Cal - i -

for - nia to the New York is - land; from the red - wood

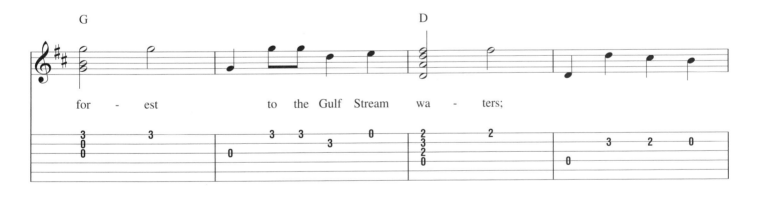

for - est to the Gulf Stream wa - ters;

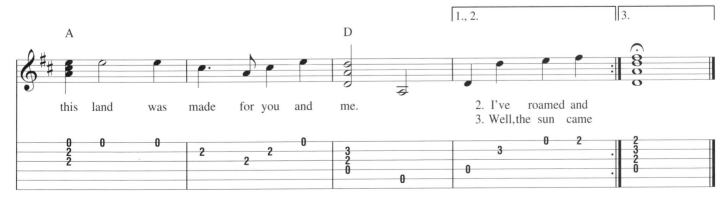

this land was made for you and me.

2. I've roamed and
3. Well, the sun came

173

Tomorrow

from the Musical Production ANNIE

Lyric by Martin Charnin
Music by Charles Strouse

Bridge

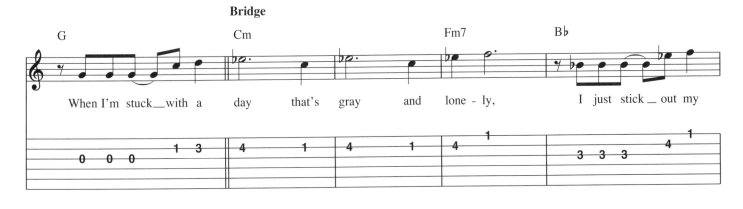

When I'm stuck—with a day that's gray and lone - ly, I just stick — out my

chin _____ and grin _____ and say: _____ 3. Oh! The

Verse

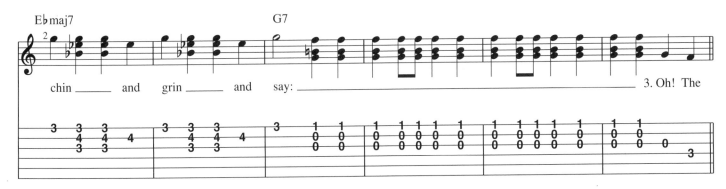

sun - 'll come out _____ to - mor - row, so you got to hang on till to -

Outro

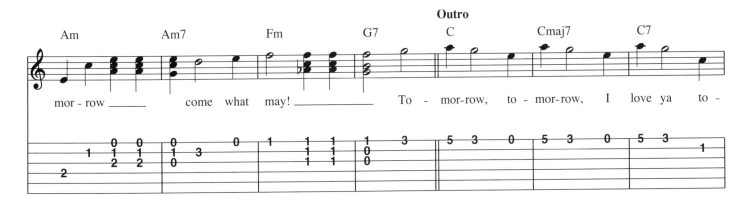

mor - row _____ come what may! _____ To - mor-row, to - mor-row, I love ya to -

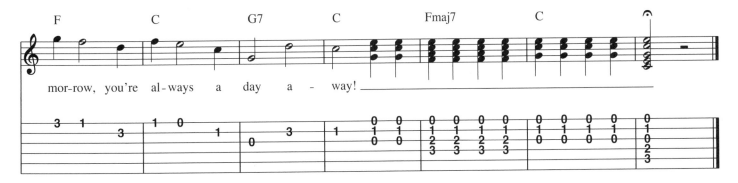

mor-row, you're al - ways a day a - way! _____

Under the Sea

from Walt Disney's THE LITTLE MERMAID
from Walt Disney's THE LITTLE MERMAID - A Broadway Musical

Music by Alan Menken
Lyrics by Howard Ashman

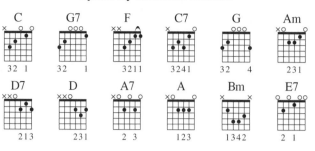

Strum Pattern: 3
Pick Pattern: 3

Intro
Moderately, in 2

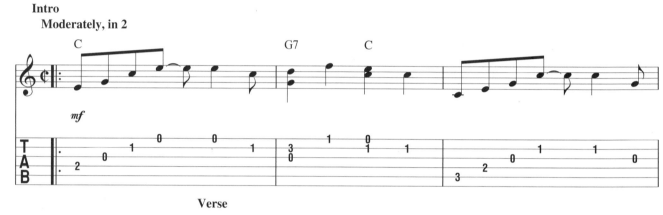

Verse

1. The sea - weed is al - ways green - er
2. Down here all is the fish is hap - py

in some - bod - y else - 's lake. You dream a - bout
as off through the wave they roll. The fish on the

go - ing up there, but that is a big mis - take.
land ain't hap - py; they sad 'cause they in the bowl.

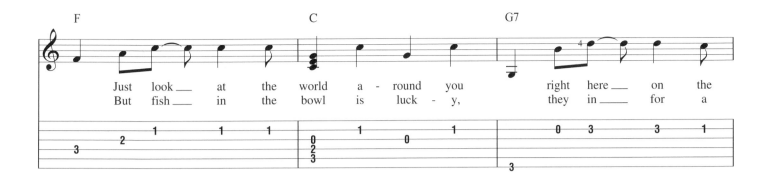

Just look ___ at the world a - round you right here ___ on the
But fish ___ in the bowl is luck - y, they in ___ for a

o - cean floor. Such won - der - ful things sur - round you.
wor - ser fate. One day ___ when the boss get hun - gry,

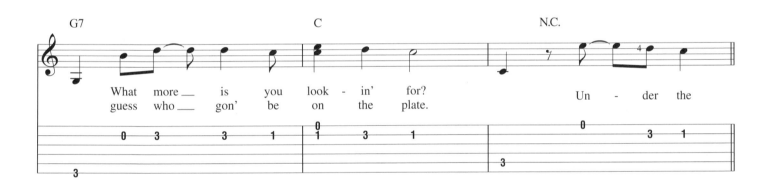

What more ___ is you look - in' for? Un - der the
guess who ___ gon' be on the plate.

𝄋 Chorus

sea, un - der the sea. Dar - lin', it's
No - bod - y
4th time, Instrumental Since ___ life is

bet - ter down ___ where it's wet - ter. Take ___ it from me.
beat us, fry ___ us and eat us in ___ fric - as - see.
sweet here, we ___ got the beat here, nat - u - ral - ly.

Up ___ on the shore they work ___ all day.
We ___ what the land they folks loves ___ to cook.
E - ven the stur - geon an' the ray,

3rd time, To Coda 1 ⊕

sun, they slave ___ a - way
sea, we off ___ the hook.
urge 'n' start ___ to play.

while ___ we de - vot - in' full ___ time to
We ___ got no trou - bles, life ___ is the
We ___ got the spir - it, you ___ got to

1.

Interlude

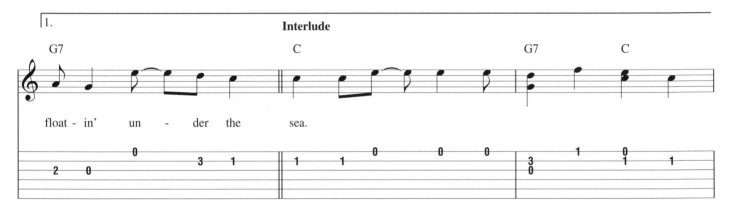

float - in' un - der the sea.

To Coda 2 ⊕   2.   *D.S. al Coda 1*

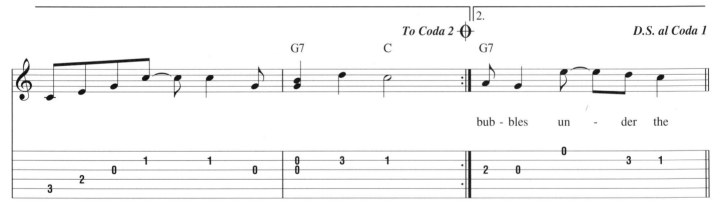

bub - bles un - der the

⊕ **Coda 1**

hear it un - der the sea.   The newt ___

Bridge

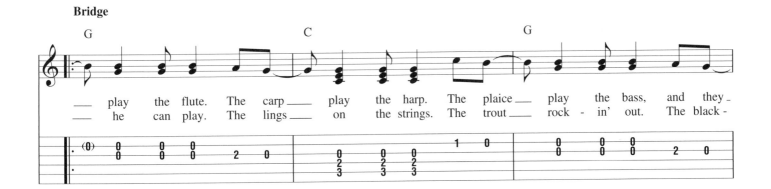

play the flute. The carp ___ play the harp. The plaice ___ play the bass, and they ___
he can play. The lings ___ on the strings. The trout ___ rock - in' out. The black-

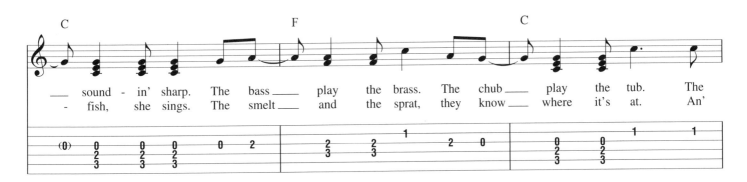

___ sound - in' sharp. The bass ___ play the brass. The chub ___ play the tub. The
- fish, she sings. The smelt ___ and the sprat, they know ___ where it's at. An'

1.   2.   *D.S. al Coda 2*
                                                                     (take 1st ending)

fluke is the duke of soul. (Yeah.) The ray, ___ blow.
oh, that ___ blow - fish

Coda 2

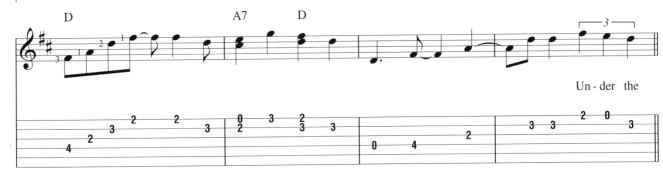

Un - der the

Outro-Chorus

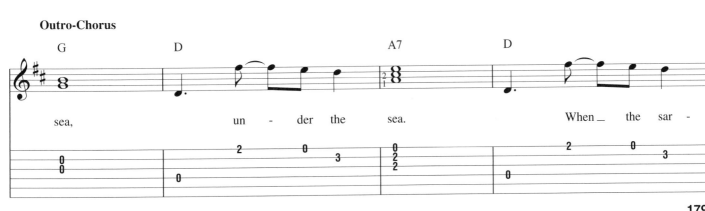

sea,   un - der the sea.   When ___ the sar -

179

dine be-gin__ the be-guine, it's mu-sic to me. What do they

got, a lot__ of sand? We got a hot crus-ta - ce-an band. Each lit-tle

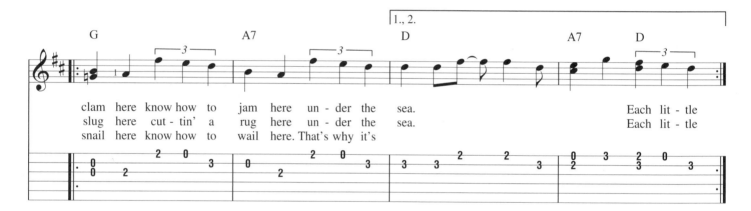

1., 2.

clam here know how to jam here un-der the sea. Each lit-tle
slug here cut-tin' a rug here un-der the sea. Each lit-tle
snail here know how to wail here. That's why it's

3.

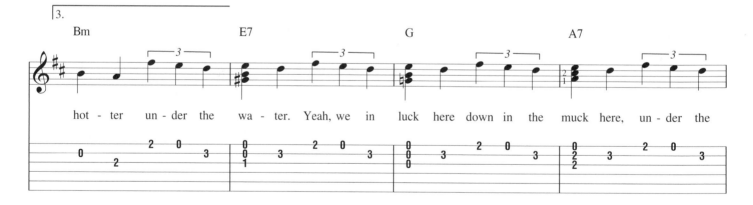

hot-ter un-der the wa-ter. Yeah, we in luck here down in the muck here, un-der the

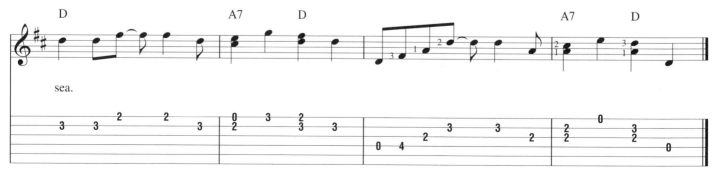

sea.

When Johnny Comes Marching Home

Words and Music by Patrick Sarsfield Gilmore

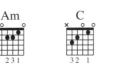

Strum Pattern: 8
Pick Pattern: 8

Moderately

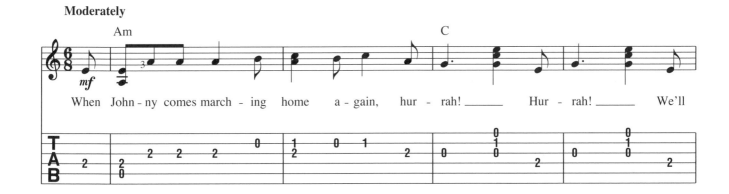

When John - ny comes march - ing home a - gain, hur - rah! _____ Hur - rah! _____ We'll

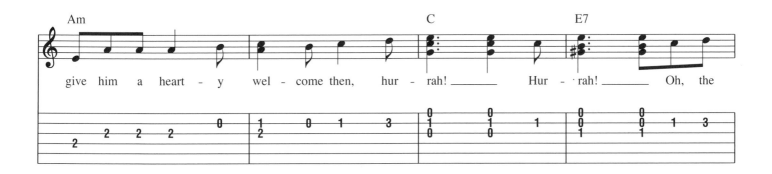

give him a heart - y wel - come then, hur - rah! _____ Hur - rah! _____ Oh, the

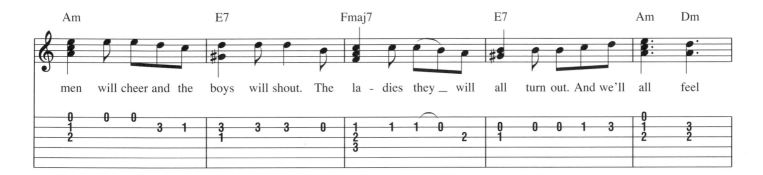

men will cheer and the boys will shout. The la - dies they _ will all turn out. And we'll all feel

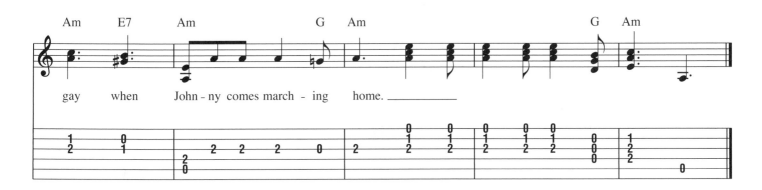

gay when John - ny comes march - ing home. _____

We're Off to See the Wizard

Lyric by E.Y. "Yip" Harburg
Music by Harold Arlen

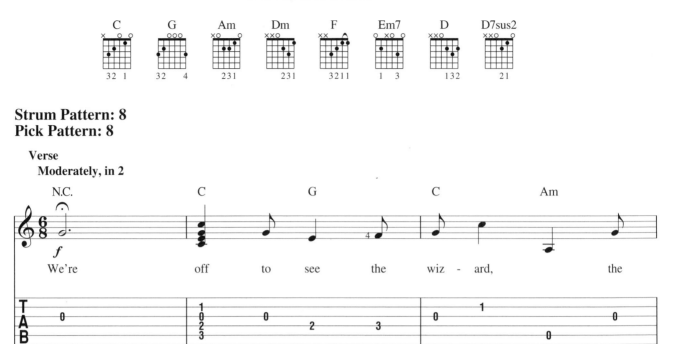

Strum Pattern: 8
Pick Pattern: 8

Verse
Moderately, in 2

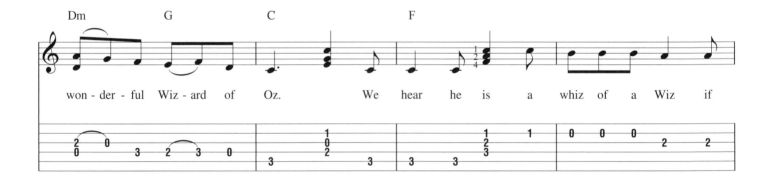

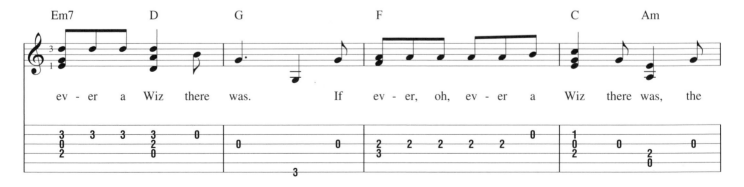

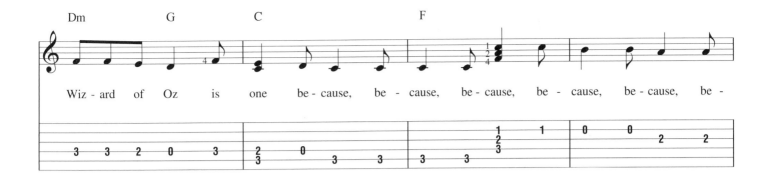

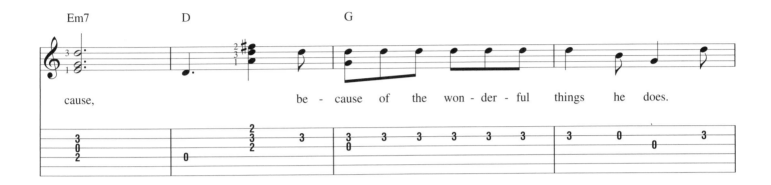

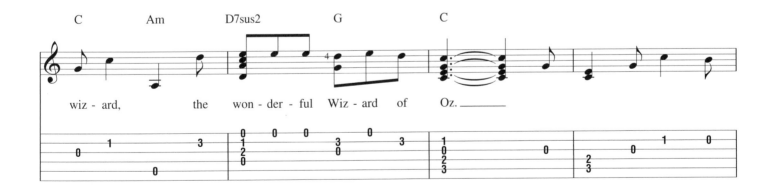

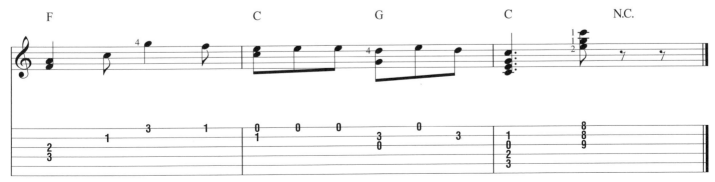

When I Grow Too Old to Dream

Lyrics by Oscar Hammerstein II
Music by Sigmund Romberg

C C#°7 G/D D#°7 Em Am7b5/Eb C/D G

B7 E A Am A/C# B7/D# F#m E/G#

G/B Am7b5 F#m7b5 F7 A7 D D7

Strum Pattern: 7
Pick Pattern: 7

Prelude
Moderately slow

C   C#°7   G/D   D#°7   Em   Am7b5/Eb

G/D   C/D   G

Intro
Moderately

G   C   G   C   G

We have been gay go- ing our way. Life has been

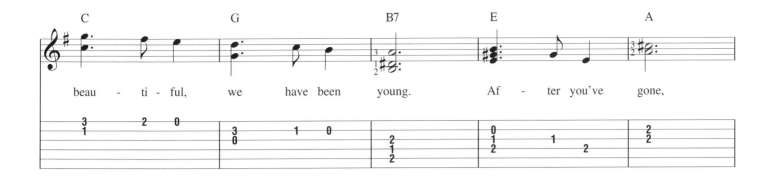

beau - ti - ful, we have been young. Af - ter you've gone,

life will go on like an old song we have

Tempo I

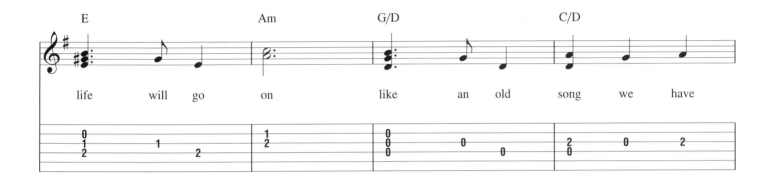

sung.

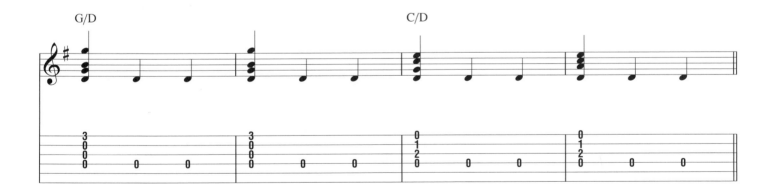

Verse

1. When I grow too old to dream,

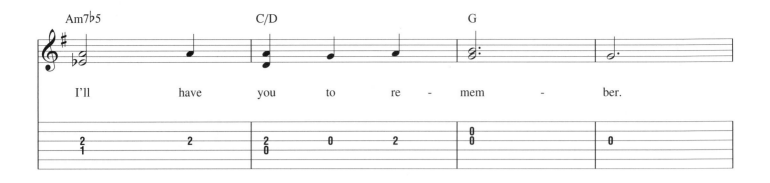

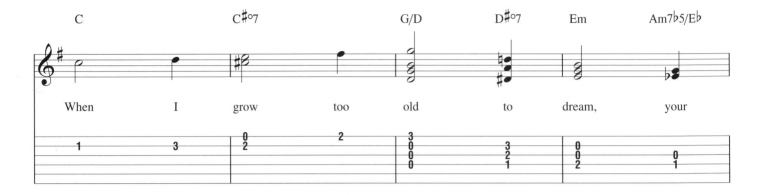

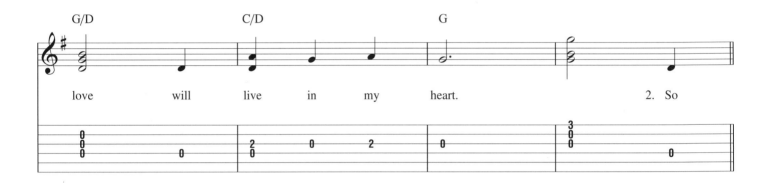

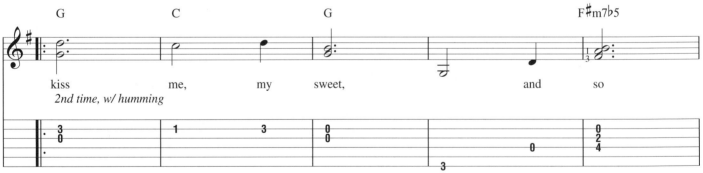

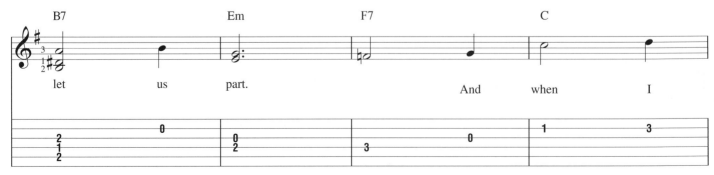

grow too old to dream, that kiss will

live in my heart. And

Outro

when I grow to old to dream, your love will

Freely

live in my heart. Oh, your love will

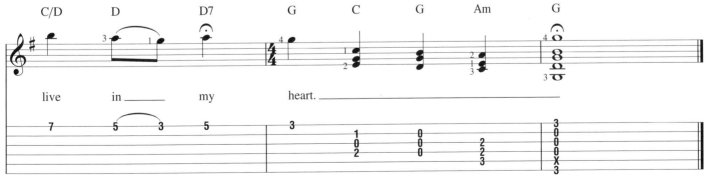

live in my heart.

When I'm Sixty-Four

from YELLOW SUBMARINE

Words and Music by John Lennon and Paul McCartney

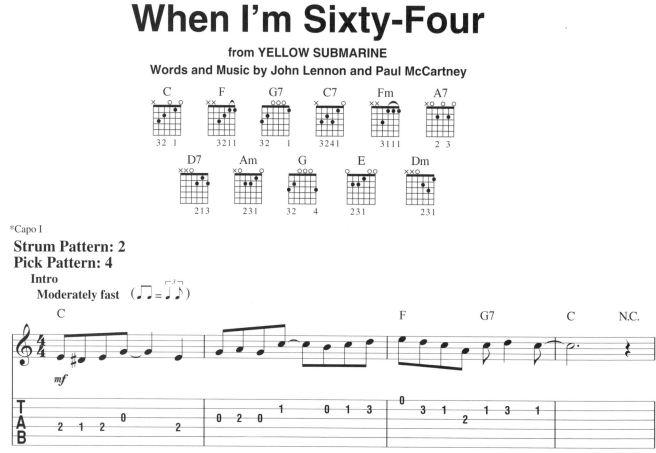

*Capo I

Strum Pattern: 2
Pick Pattern: 4

Intro
Moderately fast

*Optional: To match recording, place capo at 1st fret.

§ Verse

1. When I get old - er, los - ing my hair ___
2. I could be hand - y mend - ing a fuse ___
3. Send me a post - card, drop me a line ___

man - y years from now, ___
when your lights have gone. ___
stat - ing point of view. ___

will you still be send - ing me a
You can knit a sweat - er by the
In - di - cate pre - cise - ly what you

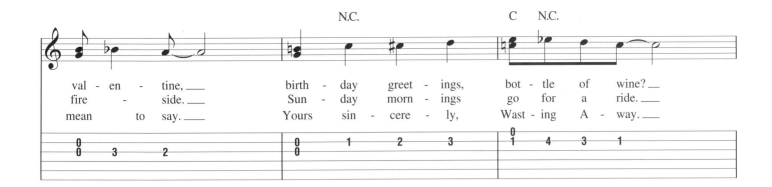

val - en - tine, ___ birth - day greet - ings, bot - tle of wine? ___
fire - side. ___ Sun - day morn - ings go for a ride. ___
mean to say. ___ Yours sin - cere - ly, Wast - ing A - way. ___

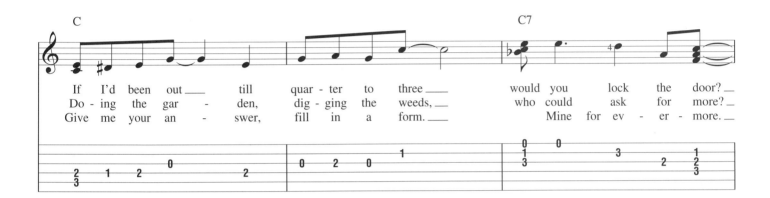

If I'd been out ___ till quar - ter to three ___ would you lock the door? ___
Do - ing the gar - den, dig - ging the weeds, ___ who could ask for more? ___
Give me your an - swer, fill in a form. ___ Mine for ev - er - more. ___

___ Will you still need ___ me, will you still feed ___ me

To Coda 1
To Coda 2

Bridge

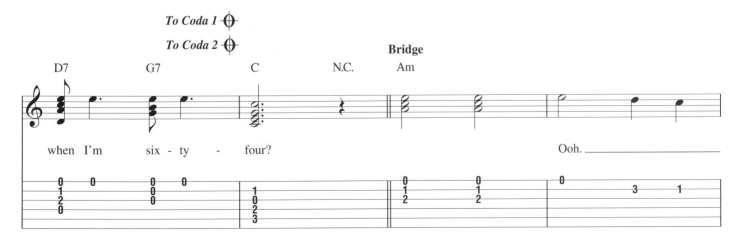

when I'm six - ty - four? Ooh. ___

You'll be old – er too. _____

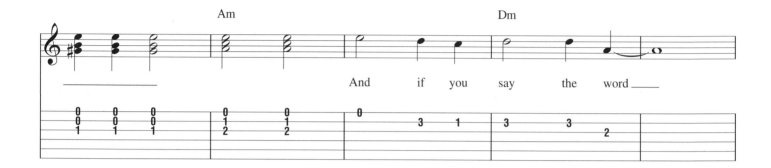

And if you say the word _____

D.S. al Coda 1

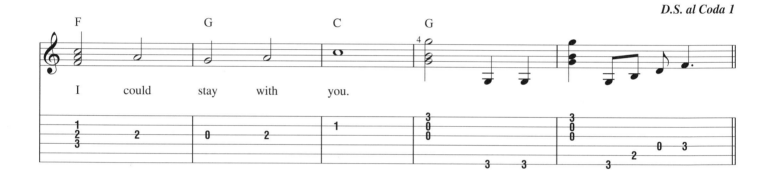

I could stay with you.

 Coda 1

Bridge

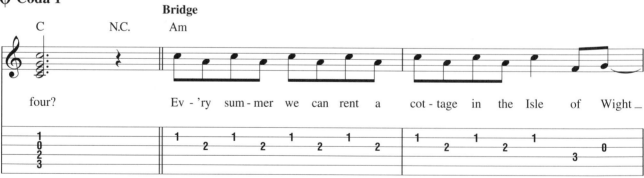

four? Ev – 'ry sum – mer we can rent a cot – tage in the Isle of Wight ___

___ if it's not too dear. ___ We shall scrimp and

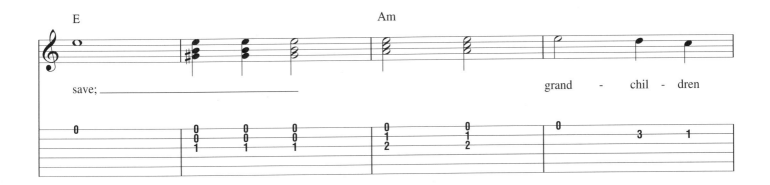

save;   grand - chil - dren

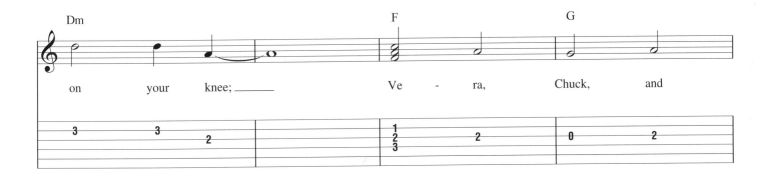

on   your   knee;   Ve - ra,   Chuck,   and

D.S. al Coda 2   **Coda 2**

Dave.   four?   Hoo!

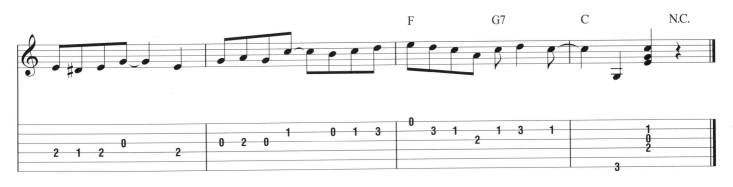

When She Loved Me

from Walt Disney Pictures' TOY STORY 2 - A Pixar Film

Music and Lyrics by Randy Newman

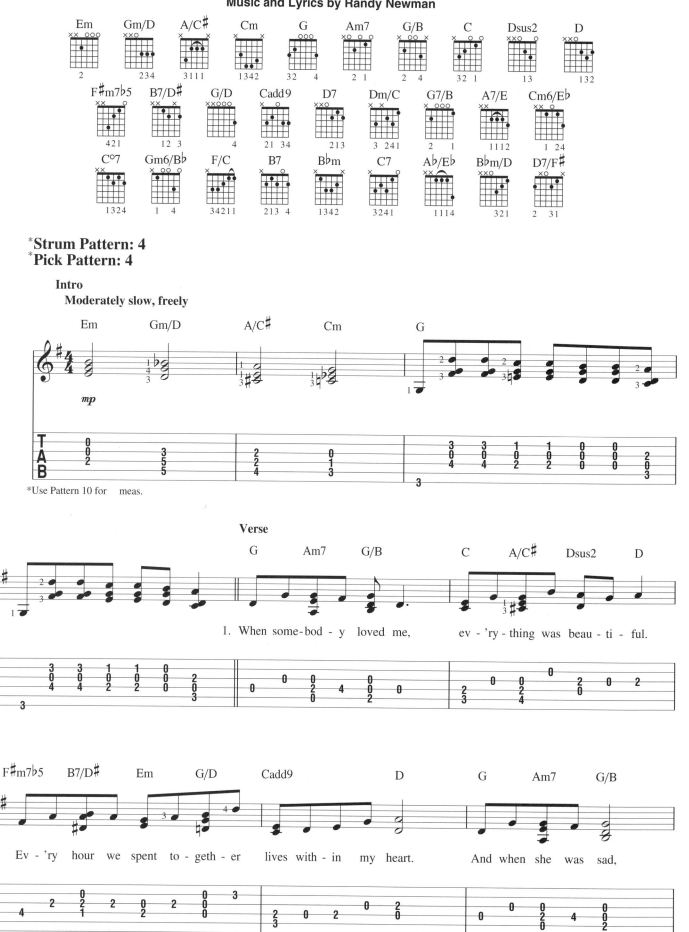

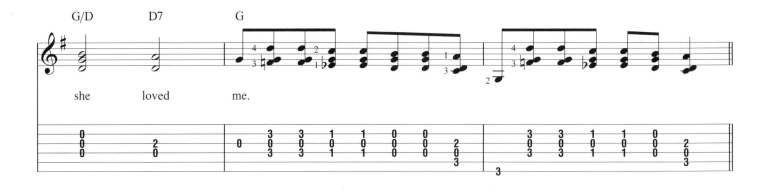

she   loved   me.

Bridge

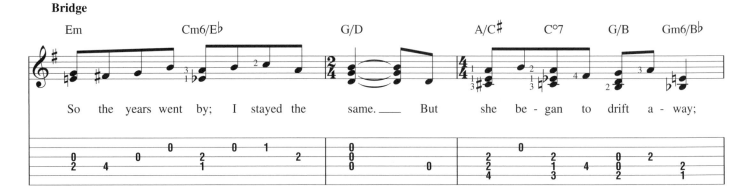

So the years went by; I stayed the   same. ___ But   she be - gan to drift a - way;

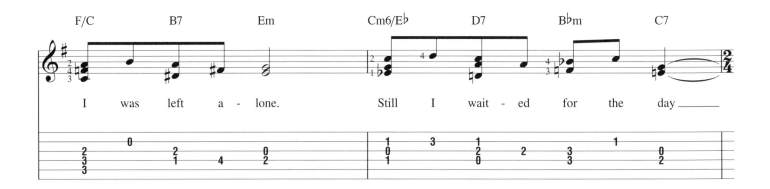

I   was   left   a - lone.   Still   I   wait - ed   for   the   day _____

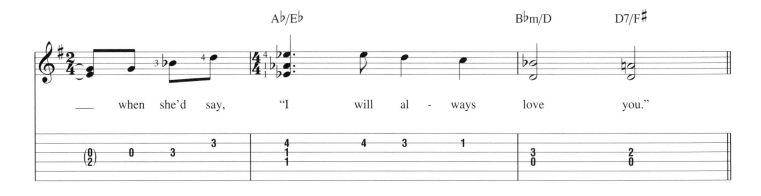

___   when she'd say,   "I   will   al - ways   love   you."

Verse

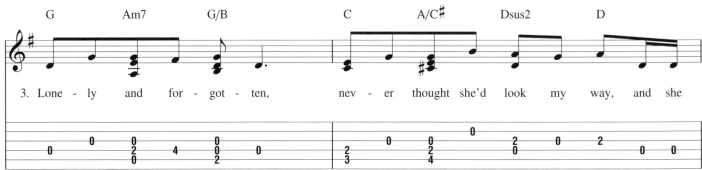

3. Lone - ly   and   for - got - ten,   nev - er   thought she'd   look   my   way,   and she

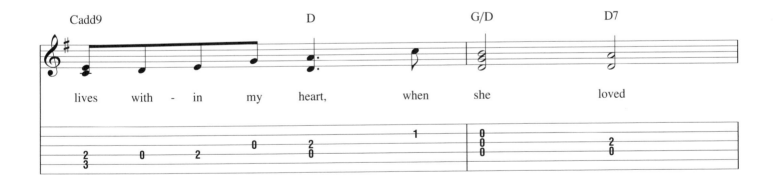

When You Wish Upon a Star

Words by Ned Washington
Music by Leigh Harline

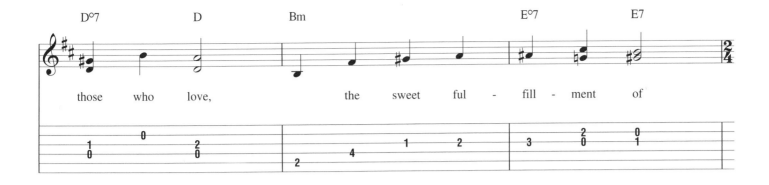

those who love, the sweet ful - fill - ment of

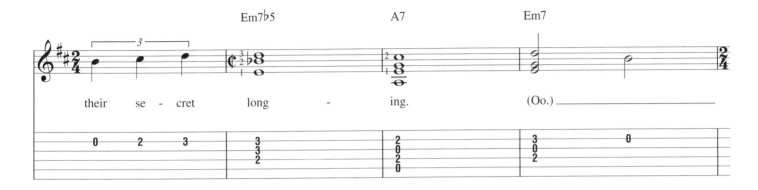

their se - cret long - ing. (Oo.) _____

Outro-Verse

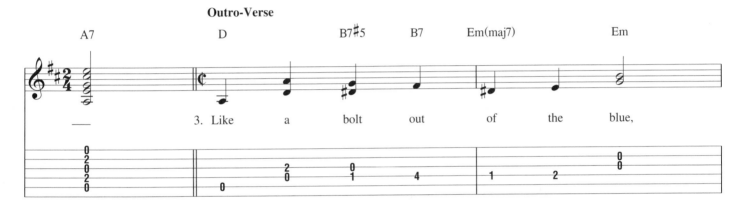

_____ 3. Like a bolt out of the blue,

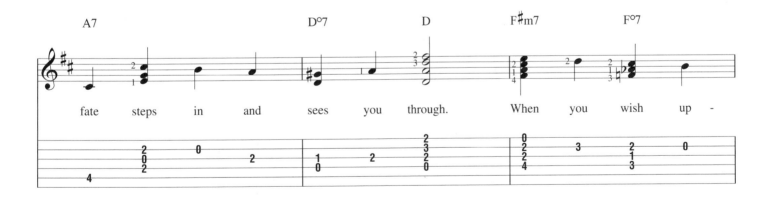

fate steps in and sees you through. When you wish up -

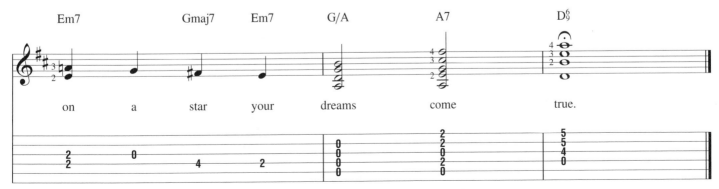

on a star your dreams come true.

Where Is Love?

from the Columbia Pictures-Romulus Film OLIVER!

Words and Music by Lionel Bart

Strum Pattern: 3
Pick Pattern: 3

Additional Lyrics

2. Where is she, who I close my eyes to see?
Will I ever know the sweet "Hello"
That's meant for only me?

4. Ev'ry night I kneel and pray:
Let tomorrow be the day
When I see the face of
Someone who I can mean something to.
Where, where is love?

You've Got a Friend in Me

from Walt Disney's TOY STORY
from Walt Disney Pictures' TOY STORY 2 - A Pixar Film
from Walt Disney Pictures' TOY STORY 3 - A Pixar Film

Music and Lyrics by Randy Newman

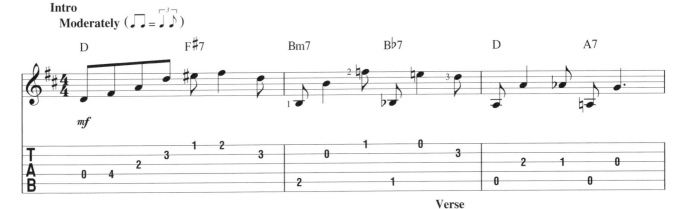

Strum Pattern: 3
Pick Pattern: 3

Intro
Moderately

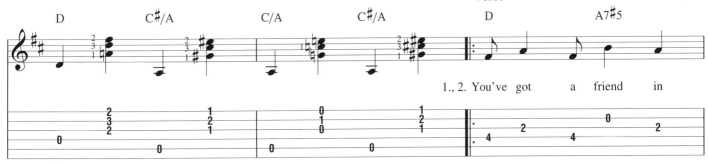

Verse

1., 2. You've got a friend in

me. You've got a friend in me.

When the road looks rough ahead and you're miles and miles from your nice
You got troubles, then I got 'em too. There isn't any-thing I

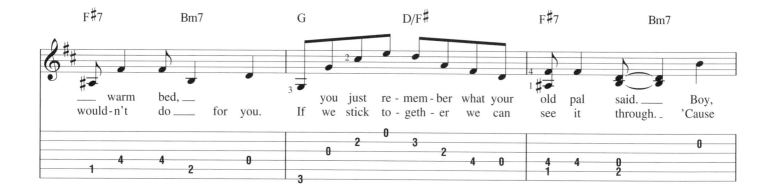

warm bed, ___ for you.
would-n't do ___ for you. If we stick to-geth-er we can see it through. ___ 'Cause

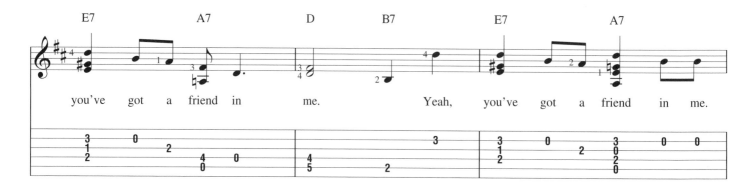

you've got a friend in me. Yeah, you've got a friend in me.

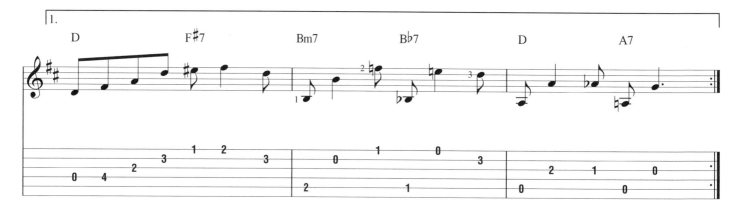

1.

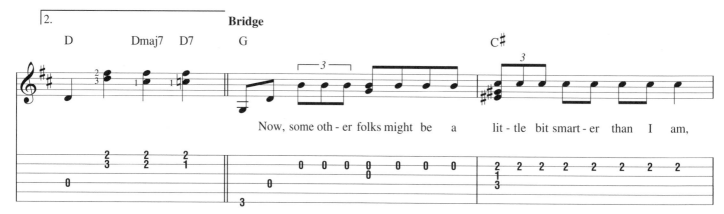

2. Bridge

Now, some oth-er folks might be a lit-tle bit smart-er than I am,

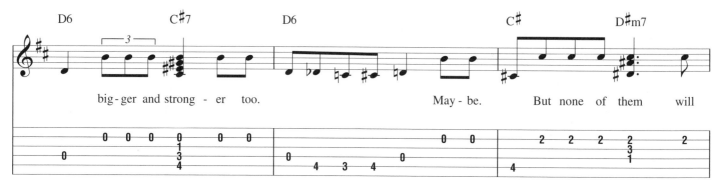

big-ger and strong-er too. May-be. But none of them will

ev - er love you the way __ I do, just me and you, __ boy.

Verse

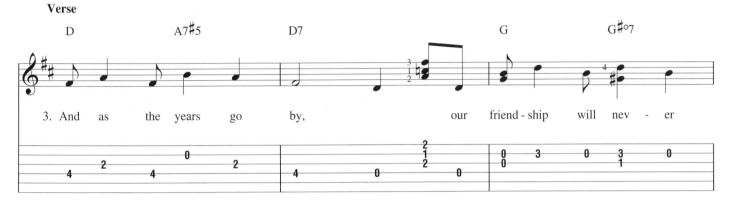

3. And as the years go by, our friend - ship will nev - er

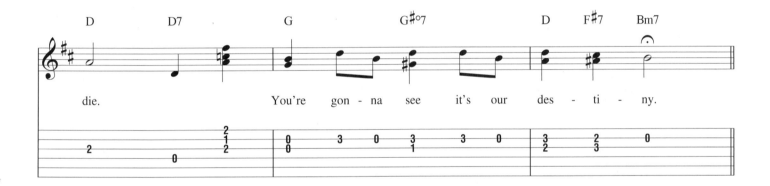

die. You're gon - na see it's our des - ti - ny.

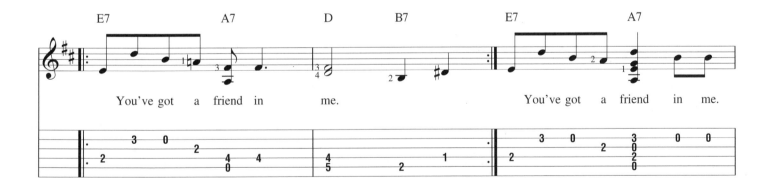

You've got a friend in me. You've got a friend in me.

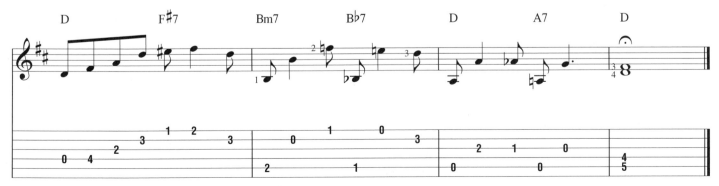

Whistle While You Work

Words by Larry Morey
Music by Frank Churchill

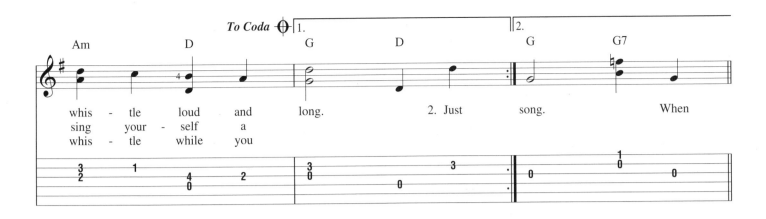

whis - tle loud and long. 2. Just song. When
sing your - self a
whis - tle while you

Bridge

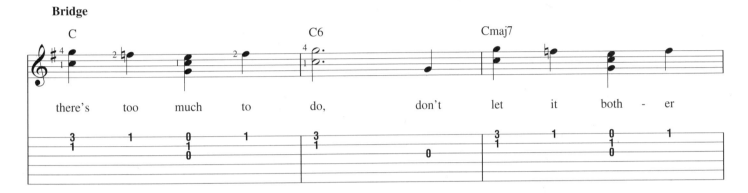

there's too much to do, don't let it both - er

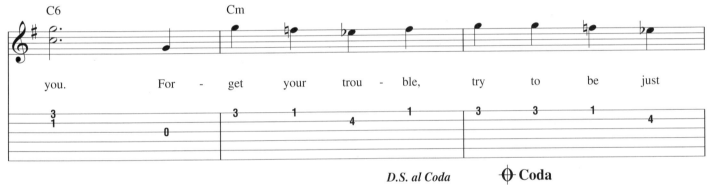

you. For - get your trou - ble, try to be just

D.S. al Coda

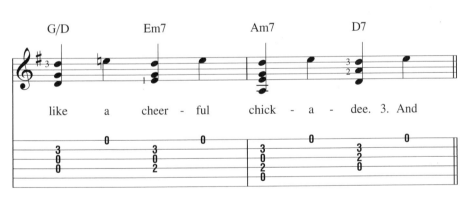

like a cheer - ful chick - a - dee. 3. And

Coda
Outro

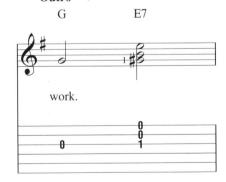

work.

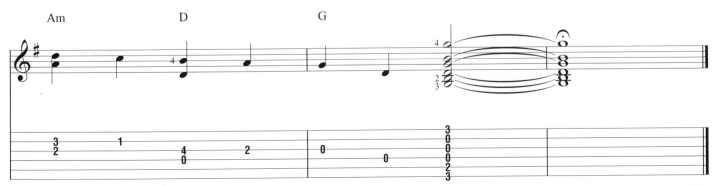

Who Will Buy?

from the Columbia Pictures-Romulus Film OLIVER!

Words and Music by Lionel Bart

Strum Pattern: 3
Pick Pattern: 2

Intro
Moderately, in 2

Chorus

1., 2. Who will
3. Who will

buy this won-der-ful morn – ing? Such a sky you nev-er did see. _____
buy this won-der-ful feel – ing? I'm so high, I swear I could fly. _____

To Coda

Who will tie it up with a rib – bon, and put it in a box for
Me, oh, my, I don't want to lose ___ it, so what am I to do to

2nd time, D.S. al Coda

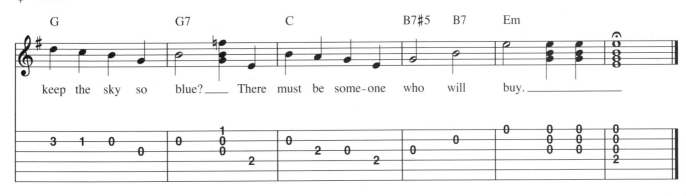

⊕ **Coda**

Additional Lyrics

2. There'll never be a day so sunny,
It could not happen twice.
Where is the man with all the money?
It's cheap at half the price!

A Whole New World

from Walt Disney's ALADDIN

Music by Alan Menken
Lyrics by Tim Rice

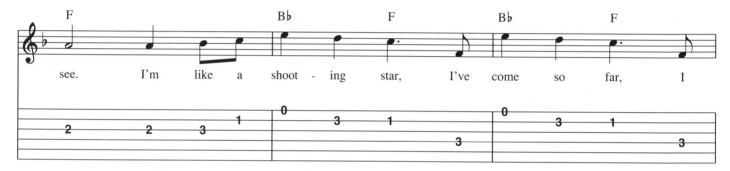

208

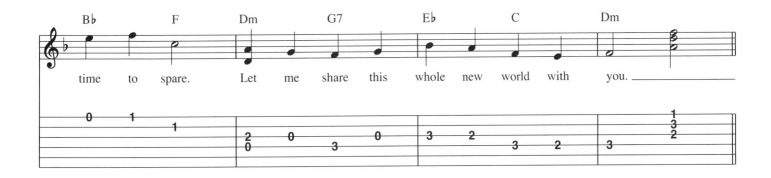

time to spare. Let me share this whole new world with you. _____

Outro

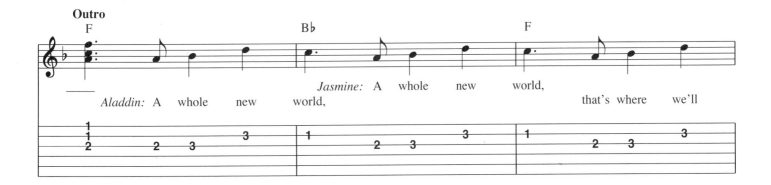

_____ *Aladdin:* A whole new world, *Jasmine:* A whole new world, that's where we'll

be. that's where we'll be. A thrill - ing chase A won - d'rous

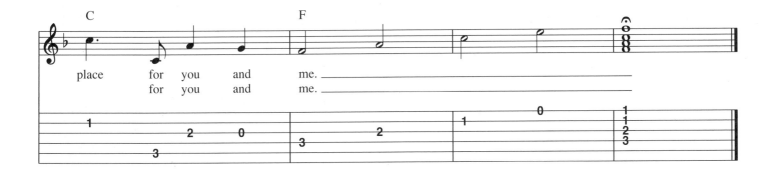

place for you and me. _____
for you and me. _____

Additional Lyrics

2. I can open your eyes,
   Take you wonder by wonder.
   Over, sideways and under
   On a magic carpet ride.

Won't You Be My Neighbor?
(It's a Beautiful Day in the Neighborhood)

from MR. ROGERS' NEIGHBORHOOD

Words and Music by Fred Rogers

*Strum Pattern: 5
*Pick Pattern: 6

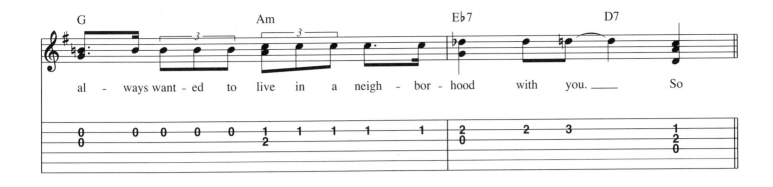

al - ways want - ed to live in a neigh - bor - hood with you. ____ So

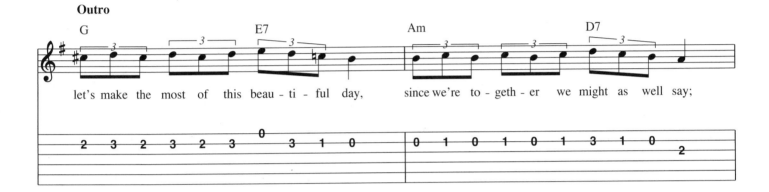

Outro

let's make the most of this beau - ti - ful day, since we're to - geth - er we might as well say;

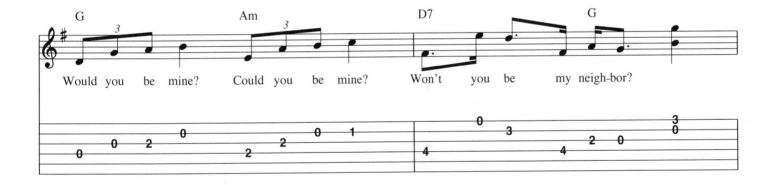

Would you be mine? Could you be mine? Won't you be my neigh-bor?

Won't you please, won't you please? Please won't you be my neigh-bor?

Chorus

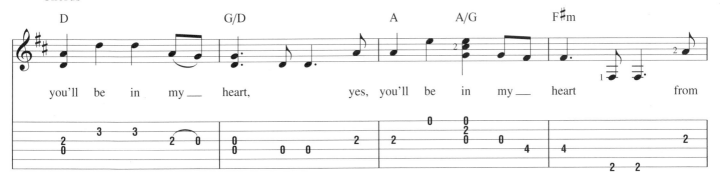

you'll be in my — heart, yes, you'll be in my — heart from

To Coda

this day on ___ now ___ and for - ev - er - more.

You'll be in my ___ heart no mat - ter what they ___

say. You'll be here in my ___ heart al - ways.

D.S. al Coda
(take 2nd ending)

Coda

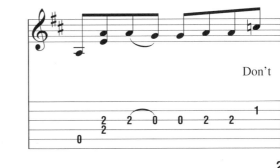

Don't

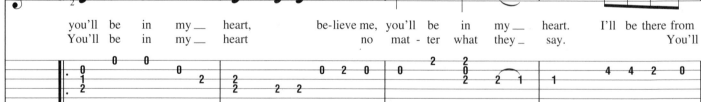

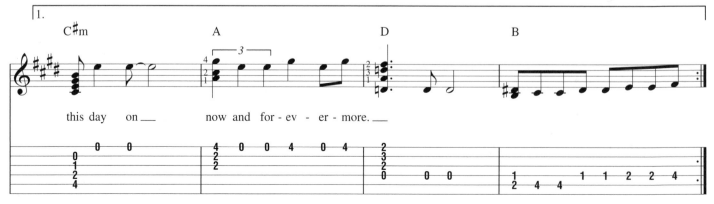

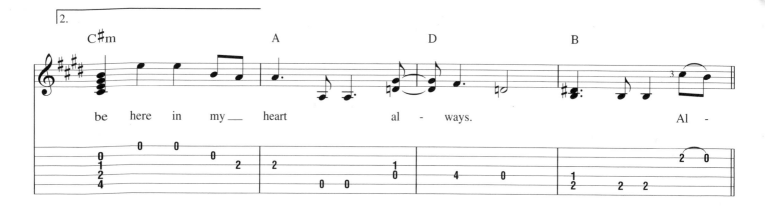

Outro

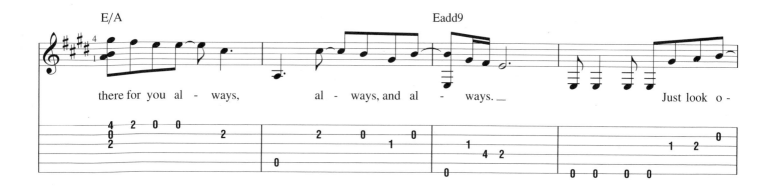

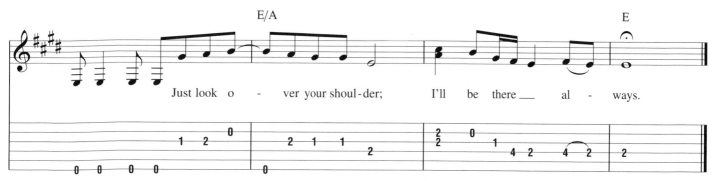

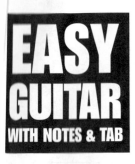

EASY GUITAR
WITH NOTES & TAB

This series features simplified arrangements with notes, tab, chord charts, and strum and pick patterns.

MIXED FOLIOS

00702287 Acoustic $14.99	00702240 Country Hits of 2007–2008 ....$12.95	00702269 1980s Rock $14.99
00702002 Acoustic Rock Hits for Easy Guitar $12.95	00702225 Country Hits of '06–'07 ....$12.95	00702268 1990s Rock $14.99
00702166 All-Time Best Guitar Collection $19.99	00702085 Disney Movie Hits $12.95	00109725 Once $14.99
00699665 Beatles Best $12.95	00702257 Easy Acoustic Guitar Songs $14.99	00702187 Selections from
00702232 Best Acoustic Songs for Easy Guitar $12.99	00702280 Easy Guitar Tab White Pages $29.99	O Brother Where Art Thou? $12.95
00702233 Best Hard Rock Songs $14.99	00702212 Essential Christmas $9.95	00702178 100 Songs for Kids........................$12.95
00703055 The Big Book of Nursery Rhymes	00702041 Favorite Hymns for Easy Guitar $9.95	00702515 Pirates of the Caribbean $12.99
& Children's Songs $14.99	00702281 4 Chord Rock $9.99	00702125 Praise and Worship for Guitar $9.95
00322179 The Big Easy Book	00702286 Glee $16.99	00702155 Rock Hits for Guitar........................$9.95
of Classic Rock Guitar $24.95	00699374 Gospel Favorites............................$14.95	00702285 Southern Rock Hits $12.99
00698978 Big Christmas Collection....................$16.95	00702160 The Great American Country Songbook..$15.99	00702866 Theme Music $12.99
00702394 Bluegrass Songs for Easy Guitar $12.99	00702050 Great Classical Themes for Easy Guitar.....$6.95	00121535 30 Easy Celtic Guitar Solos $14.99
00703387 Celtic Classics $14.99	00702116 Greatest Hymns for Guitar $8.95	00702124 Today's Christian Rock – 2nd Edition $9.95
00118314 Chart Hits of 2012-2013 ....$14.99	00702130 The Groovy Years $9.95	00702220 Today's Country Hits $9.95
00702149 Children's Christian Songbook.............$7.95	00702184 Guitar Instrumentals $9.95	00702198 Today's Hits for Guitar $9.95
00702237 Christian Acoustic Favorites $12.95	00702046 Hits of the '70s for Easy Guitar $8.95	00702217 Top Christian Hits $12.95
00702028 Christmas Classics $7.95	00702273 Irish Songs $12.99	00702235 Top Christian Hits of '07–'08.................$14.95
00101779 Christmas Guitar $14.99	00702275 Jazz Favorites for Easy Guitar $14.99	00103626 Top Hits of 2012 ....$14.99
00702185 Christmas Hits............................$9.95	00702274 Jazz Standards for Easy Guitar $14.99	00702294 Top Worship Hits $14.99
00702016 Classic Blues for Easy Guitar.............$12.95	00702162 Jumbo Easy Guitar Songbook $19.95	00702206 Very Best of Rock $9.95
00702141 Classic Rock $8.95	00702258 Legends of Rock $14.99	00702255 VH1's 100 Greatest Hard Rock Songs $27.99
00702203 CMT's 100 Greatest Country Songs $27.95	00702261 Modern Worship Hits $14.99	00702175 VH1's 100 Greatest Songs
00702283 The Contemporary	00702189 MTV's 100 Greatest Pop Songs $24.95	of Rock and Roll..................$24.95
Christian Collection $16.99	00702272 1950s Rock $14.99	00702253 Wicked $12.99
00702006 Contemporary Christian Favorites.............$9.95	00702271 1960s Rock $14.99	
00702239 Country Classics for Easy Guitar $19.99	00702270 1970s Rock $14.99	
00702282 Country Hits of 2009–2010 ....$14.99		

ARTIST COLLECTIONS

00702267 AC/DC for Easy Guitar $15.99	00702136 Best of Merle Haggard.......................$12.99	00702208 Red Hot Chili Peppers — Greatest Hits..$12.95
00702598 Adele for Easy Guitar $14.99	00702243 Hannah Montana $14.95	00702093 Rolling Stones Collection $17.95
00702001 Best of Aerosmith $16.95	00702227 Jimi Hendrix — Smash Hits $14.99	00702092 Best of the Rolling Stones $14.99
00702040 Best of the Allman Brothers.................$14.99	00702288 Best of Hillsong United $12.99	00702196 Best of Bob Seger $12.95
00702865 J.S. Bach for Easy Guitar $12.99	00702236 Best of Antonio Carlos Jobim $12.95	00702252 Frank Sinatra — Nothing But the Best ..$12.99
00702169 Best of The Beach Boys $12.99	00702245 Elton John —	00702010 Best of Rod Stewart $14.95
00702292 The Beatles — 1 ....$19.99	Greatest Hits 1970–2002 ....$14.99	00702049 Best of George Strait $12.95
00702201 The Essential Black Sabbath $12.95	00702204 Robert Johnson $9.95	00702259 Taylor Swift for Easy Guitar $14.99
00702140 Best of Brooks & Dunn........................$10.95	00702277 Best of Jonas Brothers $14.99	00702260 Taylor Swift — Fearless $12.99
02501615 Zac Brown Band — The Foundation $16.99	00702234 Selections from Toby Keith —	00115960 Taylor Swift — Red $16.99
02501621 Zac Brown Band —	35 Biggest Hits $12.95	00702290 Taylor Swift — Speak Now $14.99
You Get What You Give $16.99	00702003 Kiss $9.95	00702223 Chris Tomlin — Arriving.......................$12.95
00702095 Best of Mariah Carey $12.95	00702193 Best of Jennifer Knapp $12.95	00702262 Chris Tomlin Collection $14.99
00702043 Best of Johnny Cash $16.99	00702216 Lynyrd Skynyrd $15.99	00702226 Chris Tomlin — See the Morning........$12.95
00702033 Best of Steven Curtis Chapman $14.95	00702182 The Essential Bob Marley $12.95	00702427 U2 — 18 Singles $14.99
00702291 Very Best of Coldplay $12.99	00702346 Bruno Mars —	00702108 Best of Stevie Ray Vaughan $10.95
00702263 Best of Casting Crowns $12.99	Doo-Wops & Hooligans $12.99	00702123 Best of Hank Williams $12.99
00702090 Eric Clapton's Best $10.95	00702248 Paul McCartney — All the Best $14.99	00702111 Stevie Wonder — Guitar Collection..........$9.95
00702086 Eric Clapton —	00702129 Songs of Sarah McLachlan....................$12.95	00702228 Neil Young — Greatest Hits $15.99
from the Album Unplugged....................$10.95	02501316 Metallica — Death Magnetic $15.95	00119133 Neil Young — Harvest $14.99
00702202 The Essential Eric Clapton $12.95	00702209 Steve Miller Band —	00702188 Essential ZZ Top $10.95
00702250 blink-182 — Greatest Hits $12.99	Young Hearts (Greatest Hits)...........$12.95	
00702053 Best of Patsy Cline.........................$10.95	00702096 Best of Nirvana $14.95	
00702229 The Very Best of	00702211 The Offspring — Greatest Hits $12.95	
Creedence Clearwater Revival.................$14.99	00702030 Best of Roy Orbison........................$12.95	
00702145 Best of Jim Croce $12.99	00702144 Best of Ozzy Osbourne........................$14.99	
00702278 Crosby, Stills & Nash $12.99	00702279 Tom Petty $12.99	
00702219 David Crowder*Band Collection $12.95	00102911 Pink Floyd $16.99	
00702122 The Doors for Easy Guitar $12.99	00702139 Elvis Country Favorites.....................$9.95	
00702276 Fleetwood Mac —	00702293 The Very Best of Prince $12.99	
Easy Guitar Collection $12.99	00699415 Best of Queen for Guitar $14.99	
00702190 Best of Pat Green $19.95	00109279 Best of R.E.M. $14.99	

HAL•LEONARD® CORPORATION

7777 W. BLUEMOUND RD. P.O. BOX 13819 MILWAUKEE, WI 53213

Visit Hal Leonard online at
www.halleonard.com

0713